No Ordinary Man

2005

Contents

Foreword

ANDY FROST

Jesus – the most controversial person in history – born 2000 years ago and still stirring up debate today.

Who is Jesus to you? Maybe you conjure up an image of a sandal wearing, bearded eccentric or perhaps a cool, confident philosopher? Everyone seems to have their own view but few have read his story.

When I read about the life of Jesus, my perceptions of him were radically changed. I now picture Jesus as a revolutionary. He captivated crowds. He told profound stories. He turned peoples' values upside down. He healed the sick. He calmed the storm. He drove out demons. He raised the dead. He spent time with the rich. He hung out with the poor. He sweated blood as he prayed. And then he died a revolutionary's death.

His revolution wasn't political or social but a revolution of the human heart. His revolution continues today. Speaking personally, my heart has been transformed by this extraordinary man...

So, who is this Jesus to you? Don't just take others' opinions – search it out for yourself. Take time to read Luke's account of the life of Jesus, written by someone who was close to the action.

ANDY

Andy Frost lives in London, where he works for Share Jesus International. He is involved in pioneering new styles of making Jesus known within surf, skate and club culture.

10 facts about Jesus

1. He lived rough

2. He kept company with taxmen and revolutionaries

3. One of his friends used to be a hooker

4. He said that loving people was the second most important thing in life

5. He enjoyed parties

6. He turned water into five-star wine

7. He hated hypocrisy

8. He told religious leaders they'd got it wrong

9. He was prepared to die rather than tell a lie

10. He forgave the people who abused him

IN THE BEGINNING

Many people have tried to tell the story of what God has done among us. They wrote what we had been told by the ones who were there in the beginning and saw what happened.

So I made a careful study of everything and then decided to write and tell you exactly what took place. Honourable Theophilus, I have done this to let you know the truth about what you have heard.

An Angel Tells about the Birth of John

When Herod was king of Judea, there was a priest by the name of Zechariah from the priestly group of Abijah. His wife Elizabeth was from the family of Aaron. Both of them were good people and pleased the Lord God by obeying all that he had commanded. But they didn't have children. Elizabeth couldn't have any, and both Zechariah and Elizabeth were already old.

One day Zechariah's group of priests were on duty, and he was serving God as a priest. According to the custom of the priests, he had been chosen to go into the Lord's temple* that day and to burn incense, while the people stood outside praying.

All at once an angel from the Lord appeared to Zechariah at the right side of the altar. Zechariah was confused and afraid when he saw the angel. But the angel told him:

Don't be afraid, Zechariah! God has heard your prayers. Your wife Elizabeth will have a son, and you must name him John. His birth will make you very happy, and many people will be glad. Your son will be a great servant of the Lord. He must never drink wine or beer, and the power of the Holy Spirit will be with him from the time he is born. John will lead many people in Israel to turn back to the Lord their God. He will go ahead of the Lord with the same power and spirit that Elijah had. And because of John, parents will be more thoughtful of their children. And people who now disobey God will begin to think as they ought to. That is how John will get people ready for the Lord.

Zechariah said to the angel, "How will I know this is going to happen? My wife and I are both very old."

The angel answered, "I am Gabriel, God's servant, and I was sent to tell you this good news. You haven't believed what I've said. So you won't be able to say a thing until all this happens. But everything will take place when it is supposed to."

"Nothing is impossible for God"

The crowd was waiting for Zechariah and kept wondering why he was staying so long in the temple. When he did come out, he couldn't speak, and they knew he had seen a vision. He motioned to them with his hands, but didn't say anything.

When Zechariah's time of service in the temple was over, he went home. Soon after that, his wife was expecting a baby, and for five months she didn't leave the house. She said to herself, "What the Lord has done for me will keep people from looking down on me."

An Angel Tells about the Birth of Jesus
One month later God sent the angel Gabriel to the town of Nazareth in Galilee with a message for a virgin named Mary. She was engaged to Joseph from the family of King David. The angel greeted Mary and said, "You are truly blessed! The Lord is with you."

Mary was confused by the angel's words and wondered what they meant. Then the angel told Mary, "Don't be afraid! God is pleased with you, and you will have a son. His name will be Jesus. He will be great and will be called the Son of God Most High. The Lord God will make him king, as his ancestor David was. He will rule the people of Israel for ever, and his kingdom will never end."

Mary asked the angel, "How can this happen? I'm not married!"

The angel answered, "The Holy Spirit will come down to you, and God's power will come over you. So your child will be called the holy Son of God. Your relative Elizabeth is also going to have a son, even though she is old. No one thought she could ever have a baby, but in three months she will have a son. Nothing is impossible for God!"

Mary said, "I am the Lord's servant! Let it happen as you have said." And the angel left her.

Mary Visits Elizabeth
A short time later Mary hurried to a town in the hill country of Judea. She went into Zechariah's home, where she greeted Elizabeth. When Elizabeth heard Mary's greeting, her baby moved inside her.

The Holy Spirit came upon Elizabeth. Then in a loud voice she said to Mary:

God has blessed you more than any other woman! He has also blessed the child you will have. Why should the mother of my Lord come to me? As soon as I heard your greeting, my baby became happy and moved inside me. The Lord has blessed you because you believed that he will keep his promise.

Mary's Song of Praise
Mary said:
>With all my heart
>I praise the Lord,
>and I am glad
>because of God my Saviour.
>He cares for me,
>his humble servant.
>From now on,
>all people will say

* TEMPLE
The temple in Jerusalem was the national centre of worship for the Jews. Built by Herod the Great, it was destroyed by the Romans in AD70. Luke records Jesus' prophecy of its destruction (see page 60).

WHO WROTE THIS ACCOUNT OF JESUS?

Luke, an educated Greek, wrote his account because as a follower of Jesus he wanted to tell people about his faith. His Gospel is dedicated to Theophilus, who was probably an important Roman official, perhaps even a Christian himself.

Luke begins his Gospel like a history book of the time, with a formal address, stating the sources he used. He explains that he intends to write a well-organised and researched account of the life of Jesus, based on reliable reports and eye-witness accounts. He is claiming to write history – as accurate as any other produced in the ancient world. Where his information can be checked we find that he accurately describes geography, cultural details and the complex situations of the time.

Luke probably never met Jesus, but historians believe he met Mark (who also wrote a Gospel) and some think he talked to Jesus' mother, Mary, to gain information. He wrote his book about thirty years after the death of Jesus, when many of the people who knew Jesus personally were still alive.

Did Jesus really live? See page 16.

See the Evidence pages in the Question and Answer section on www.rejesus.co.uk/the_story

God has blessed me.
God All-Powerful has done
great things for me,
and his name is holy.
He always shows mercy
to everyone
who worships him.
The Lord has used
his powerful arm
to scatter those
who are proud.
He drags strong rulers
from their thrones
and puts humble people
in places of power.
God gives the hungry
good things to eat,
and sends the rich away
with nothing.
He helps his servant Israel
and is always merciful
to his people.
The Lord made this promise
to our ancestors,
to Abraham and his family
for ever!

Mary stayed with Elizabeth about three months. Then she went back home.

The Birth of John the Baptist

When Elizabeth's son was born, her neighbours and relatives heard how kind the Lord had been to her, and they too were glad.

Eight days later they did for the child what the Law of Moses commands. They were going to name him Zechariah, after his father. But Elizabeth said, "No! His name is John."

The people argued, "No one in your family has ever been named John." So they motioned to Zechariah to find out what he wanted to name his son.

Zechariah asked for a writing tablet. Then he wrote, "His name is John." Everyone was amazed. Straight away, Zechariah started speaking and praising God.

All the neighbours were frightened because of what had happened, and

"Don't be afraid! I have good news for you."

everywhere in the hill country people kept talking about these things. Everyone who heard about this wondered what this child would grow up to be. They knew that the Lord was with him.

Zechariah Praises the Lord

The Holy Spirit came upon Zechariah, and he began to speak:
Praise the Lord,
the God of Israel!
He has come
to save his people.
Our God has given us
a mighty Saviour
from the family
of David his servant.
Long ago the Lord
promised
by the words
of his holy prophets
to save us from our
enemies
and from everyone
who hates us.
God said he would be kind
to our people
and keep
his sacred promise.
He told our ancestor
Abraham
that he would rescue us

from our enemies.
Then we could serve him
without fear,
by being holy and good
as long as we live.
You, my son, will be called
a prophet of God
in heaven above.
You will go ahead of the
Lord
to get everything ready
for him.
You will tell his people
that they can be saved
when their sins
are forgiven.
God's love and kindness
will shine upon us
like the sun that rises
in the sky.
On us who live
in the dark shadow
of death
this light will shine
to guide us
into a life of peace.

As John grew up, God's
Spirit gave him great
power. John lived in the
desert until the time he
was sent to the people
of Israel.

The Birth of Jesus

About that time Emperor
Augustus* gave orders for
the names of all the people
to be listed in record books.
These first records were made
when Quirinius was governor
of Syria.

Everyone had to go to
their own home town to be
listed. So Joseph had to leave
Nazareth in Galilee and go
to Bethlehem in Judea. Long
ago Bethlehem had been
King David's home town, and
Joseph went there because he
was from David's family.

Mary was engaged to
Joseph and travelled with
him to Bethlehem. She was
soon going to have a baby,
and while they were there,
she gave birth to her firstborn
son. She dressed him in baby
clothes and laid him on a bed
of hay, because there was no
room for them in the inn.

The Shepherds

That night in the fields near
Bethlehem some shepherds
were guarding their sheep. All
at once an angel came down
to them from the Lord, and the
brightness of the Lord's glory
flashed around them. The
shepherds were frightened.
But the angel said, "Don't be
afraid! I have good news for
you, which will make everyone
happy. This very day in King
David's home town a Saviour
was born for you. He is Christ
the Lord. You will know who
he is, because you will find him
dressed in baby clothes and
lying on a bed of hay."

* EMPEROR AUGUSTUS

In Jesus' time, the
Roman Empire
dominated Europe
and the Middle East.
Israel was an occupied
land, paying taxes to
Rome. Its kings, the
Herod family, were
no more than puppet
rulers. The real power
lay in the hands of the
Roman army.

"I'm terribly torn
about being born.
What is the whole
thing about?"
Victoria Wood

The Road to
Bethlehem

7

* CHRIST

Christ is a Greek word meaning a person who has been chosen by God for a special task. The Hebrew word for "Christ" is "Messiah". So "Christ" is not Jesus' surname. The Jewish scriptures promised that the Messiah would come to rescue their nation, to be their saviour. By the time of Jesus, the Jews understood that promise to mean that God would send a great military and political ruler who would raise an army and drive out the Romans. By his words and actions Jesus laid claim to be that Messiah. However, he came not as a conquering king, but as a suffering saviour.

Suddenly many other angels came down from heaven and joined in praising God. They said:

"Praise God in heaven! Peace on earth to everyone who pleases God."

After the angels had left and gone back to heaven, the shepherds said to each other, "Let's go to Bethlehem and see what the Lord has told us about." They hurried off and found Mary and Joseph, and they saw the baby lying on a bed of hay.

When the shepherds saw Jesus, they told his parents what the angel had said about him. Everyone listened and was surprised. But Mary kept thinking about all this and wondering what it meant.

As the shepherds returned to their sheep, they were praising God and saying wonderful things about him. Everything they had seen and heard was just as the angel had said.

Eight days later Jesus' parents did for him what the Law of Moses commands. And they named him Jesus, just as the angel had told Mary when he promised she would have a baby.

Simeon Praises the Lord

The time came for Mary and Joseph to do what the Law of Moses says a mother is supposed to do after her baby is born.

They took Jesus to the temple in Jerusalem and presented him to the Lord, just as the Law of the Lord says, "Each firstborn baby boy belongs to the Lord." The Law of the Lord also says that parents have to offer a sacrifice, giving at least a pair of doves or two young pigeons. So that is what Mary and Joseph did.

At this time a man named Simeon was living in Jerusalem. Simeon was a good man. He loved God and was waiting for God to save the people of Israel. God's Spirit came to him and told him that he wouldn't die until he had seen Christ* the Lord.

When Mary and Joseph brought Jesus to the temple to do what the Law of Moses says should be done for a new baby, the Spirit told Simeon to go into the temple. Simeon took the baby Jesus in his arms and praised God,

"Lord, I am your servant, and now I can die in peace, because you have kept

Life Story

ELAINE ROBERTS

"I had the most explosive temper and a vocabulary to match"

Elaine Roberts traces the beginning of a change in her life to watching the film 'Ben Hur' on Boxing Day 1982.

"I was deeply moved by the film. For two weeks afterwards I had not lost my temper or even sworn. I wondered if this was due to the effect of the film, or whether it had anything to do with God."

"I bought a Bible and got up each morning to read it and pray to a God that I wasn't even sure existed. I noticed that my prayers were answered... Coincidence?... When I prayed 'coincidences' happened, when I didn't pray, they didn't."

"I decided to have nothing more to do with astrology and to consult God and the Bible for guidance instead. I discovered the Bible to be the most fascinating and relevant book I have ever read. I found a church where they taught from the Bible about the birth, life, death, resurrection and return of Jesus Christ, and I was hooked. One particular couple, Sam and Joyce, were a great help to me."

"Jesus Christ has had an incredible impact on my life. Since becoming a Christian I have suffered a miscarriage of twins and still remain childless. Someone tried to murder my mother. A cousin was violently hacked to death. I nursed a 30 year old cousin with terminal liver cancer. And my father was killed by three youths. Yet through all these catastrophes, and all the other junk that life throws at you, I have always known the tangible strength and support of God. It was his divine strength that enabled me to forgive the people who killed my cousin and my father. Once I would have rearranged a person's face for much less."

"In addition, I know that I, too, have been forgiven by God for the way I have lived my life. I am at peace with God because I know that God loves me so much he sent his only son Jesus to die for me."

"Today I am a minister."

* JOHN THE BAPTIST

John the Baptist's role was to prepare the Jews for the coming of Jesus. He preached fearlessly and powerfully that people should turn away from their self-centredness. He was Jesus' cousin, older by six months. Apparently he didn't know Jesus personally, as John lived (as a hermit) in the Judean desert. When he attacked the corruption of King Herod, he was thrown into prison and later killed. Jesus said that John was the greatest of Israel's prophets (see pages 23 & 24).

your promise to me.
With my own eyes
I have seen
what you have done
to save your people,
and foreign nations
will also see this.
Your mighty power
is a light
for all nations,
and it will bring honour
to your people Israel."

Jesus' parents were surprised at what Simeon had said. Then he blessed them and told Mary, "This child of yours will cause many people in Israel to fall and others to stand. The child will be like a warning sign. Many people will reject him, and you, Mary, will suffer as though you had been stabbed by a dagger. But all this will show what people are really thinking."

Anna Speaks about the Child Jesus

The prophet Anna was also there in the temple. She was the daughter of Phanuel from the tribe of Asher, and she was very old. In her youth she had been married for seven years, but her husband had died. And now she was 84 years old. Night and day she served God in the temple by praying and often going without eating.

At that time Anna came in and praised God. She spoke about the child Jesus to everyone who hoped for Jerusalem to be set free.

The Return to Nazareth

After Joseph and Mary had done everything that the Law of the Lord commands, they returned home to Nazareth in Galilee. The child Jesus grew. He became strong and wise, and God blessed him.

The Boy Jesus in the Temple

Every year Jesus' parents went to Jerusalem for Passover. And when Jesus was 12 years old, they all went there as usual for the celebration. After Passover his parents left, but they didn't know that Jesus had stayed on in the city. They thought he was travelling with some other people, and they went a whole day before they started looking for him. When they couldn't find him with their relatives and friends, they went back to Jerusalem and started looking for him there.

Three days later they found Jesus sitting in the temple, listening to the teachers and asking them questions. Everyone who heard him was surprised at how much he knew and at the answers he gave.

When his parents found him, they were amazed. His mother said, "Son, why have you done this to us? Your father and I have been very worried, and we've been searching for you!"

Jesus answered, "Why did you have to look for me? Didn't you know that I would be in my Father's house?" But they didn't understand what he meant.

Jesus went back to Nazareth with his parents and obeyed them. His mother kept on thinking about all that had happened.

Jesus became wise, and he grew strong. God was pleased with him and so were the people.

The Preaching of John the Baptist*

For 15 years Emperor Tiberius had ruled that part of the world. Pontius Pilate was governor of Judea, and Herod was the ruler of Galilee. Herod's brother, Philip, was the ruler in the countries of Iturea and Trachonitis, and Lysanias was the ruler of Abilene. Annas and Caiaphas were the Jewish high priests.

At that time God spoke to Zechariah's son John, who was living in the desert. So John went along the Jordan Valley, telling the people,

"Turn back to God and be baptised! Then your sins will be forgiven." Isaiah the

NIGEL CUTLAND

Nigel Cutland is a professor of mathematics. He became a Christian when he was twenty and a student at university.

"I'd always had a vague sense that there was something there, but I didn't know who or what God was. At university I took up the offer from a fellow student to explore what Christianity was about, through discussions over coffee, listening to tapes and reading books. One which stood out was 'Mere Christianity' by C.S. Lewis, whose arguments made such perfect sense to me as a mathematician."

"I realised that the Christian faith was not about doing your best and hoping God would give you a pass mark if you had done well enough. I also understood for the first time that it was about getting right with God, not because of what I could do, but because of what he has done through Jesus' death on the cross. I was amazed to discover that God was offering me a new kind of life, like a heart transplant, so that I would begin to live his way."

"My questioning took place over a period of eighteen months to two years. Although I was convinced intellectually, I was still reluctant to make a personal commitment to God which I knew was at the heart of the Christian faith. Then God brought me to a point when I knew I had to take a step of faith, and I became a Christian."

"To have a relationship with the God of the universe has given me a real sense of purpose and security about knowing who I am and where I am going. That sense of purpose pervades my whole life. As a mathematician, knowing that what I am doing is within the framework and design of the Creator makes it very worthwhile. It's also a big help to me to know that it is God who has given us minds and has made a world which is to be investigated and discovered. Another great joy for me as a Christian is the sense of belonging to a family, people who accept and love me. It shows me that God's love is real."

prophet wrote about John when he said,

"In the desert someone is shouting, 'Get the road ready for the Lord! Make a straight path for him. Fill up every valley and level every mountain and hill. Straighten the crooked paths and smooth out the rough roads. Then everyone will see the saving power of God.'"

Crowds of people came out to be baptised, but John said to them, "You bunch of snakes! Who warned you to run from the coming judgment? Do something to show that you really have given up your sins. Don't start saying that you belong to Abraham's family. God can turn these stones into children for Abraham. An axe is ready to cut the trees down at their

"Someone more powerful is going to come"

roots. Any tree that doesn't produce good fruit will be cut down and thrown into a fire."

The crowds asked John, "What should we do?"

John told them, "If you have two coats, give one to someone who doesn't have any. If you have food, share it with someone else."

When tax collectors came to be baptised, they asked John, "Teacher, what should we do?"

John told them, "Don't make people pay more than they owe."

Some soldiers asked him, "And what about us? What do we have to do?"

John told them, "Don't force people to pay money to make you leave them alone. Be satisfied with your pay."

Everyone became excited and wondered, "Could John be the Messiah?"

John said, "I'm just baptising with water. But someone more powerful is going to come, and I'm not good enough even to untie his sandals. He will baptise you with the Holy Spirit and with fire. His threshing fork is in his hand, and he is ready to separate the wheat from the husks. He will store the wheat in his barn and burn the husks with a fire that never goes out."

In many different ways John preached the good news to the people. But to Herod the ruler, he said, "It was wrong for you to take Herodias, your brother's wife." John also said that Herod had done many other bad things. Finally, Herod put John in jail, and this was the worst thing he ever did.

The Baptism of Jesus

While everyone else was being baptised, Jesus himself was baptised. Then as he prayed, the sky opened up, and the Holy Spirit came down upon him in the form of a dove. A voice from heaven said, "You are my own dear Son, and I am pleased with you."

The Ancestors of Jesus

When Jesus began to preach, he was about 30 years old. Everyone thought he was the son of Joseph. But his family went back through Heli, Matthat, Levi, Melchi, Jannai, Joseph, Mattathias, Amos, Nahum, Esli, Naggai, Maath, Mattathias, Semein, Josech, Joda;

Joanan, Rhesa, Zerubbabel, Shealtiel, Neri, Melchi, Addi, Cosam, Elmadam, Er, Joshua, Eliezer, Jorim, Matthat, Levi;

Simeon, Judah, Joseph, Jonam, Eliakim, Melea, Menna, Mattatha, Nathan, David, Jesse, Obed, Boaz, Salmon, Nahshon;

Amminadab, Admin, Arni, Hezron, Perez, Judah, Jacob, Isaac, Abraham, Terah, Nahor, Serug, Reu, Peleg, Eber, Shelah;

Cainan, Arphaxad, Shem, Noah, Lamech, Methuselah, Enoch, Jared, Mahalaleel, Kenan, Enosh, and Seth.

The family of Jesus went all the way back to Adam and then to God.

NO ORDINARY MAN

When Jesus returned from the Jordan River, the power of the Holy Spirit was with him, and the Spirit led him into the desert. For 40 days Jesus was tested by the devil, and during that time he went without eating. When it was all over, he was hungry.

The devil said to Jesus, "If you are God's Son, tell this stone to turn into bread."

Jesus answered, "The scriptures say, 'No one can live only on food.'"

Then the devil led Jesus up to a high place and quickly showed him all the nations on earth. The devil said, "I will give all this power and glory to you. It has been given to me, and I can give it to anyone I want to. Just worship me, and you can have it all."

Jesus answered, "The Scriptures say:
'Worship the Lord your God and serve only him!'"

"No one can live only on food"

Finally, the devil took Jesus to Jerusalem and had him stand on top of the temple. The devil said, "If you are God's Son, jump off. The Scriptures say:
'God will tell his angels to take care of you.
They will catch you in their arms,
and you won't hurt your feet on the stones.'"

Jesus answered, "The Scriptures also say, 'Don't try to test the Lord your God!'"

After the devil had finished testing Jesus in every way possible, he left him for a while.

Jesus Begins His Work

Jesus returned to Galilee with the power of the Spirit. News about him spread everywhere. He taught in the Jewish meeting places, and everyone praised him.

The People of Nazareth Turn against Jesus

Jesus went back to Nazareth, where he had been brought up, and as usual he went to the meeting place on the Sabbath. When he stood up to read from the Scriptures, he was given the book of Isaiah the prophet. He opened it and read,

"The Lord's Spirit
has come to me,
because he has chosen me
to tell the good news
to the poor.
The Lord has sent me
to announce freedom
for prisoners,
to give sight to the blind,
to free everyone
who suffers,
and to say, 'This is the year
the Lord has chosen.'"

Jesus closed the book, then handed it back to the man in charge and sat down. Everyone in the meeting place looked straight at Jesus. Then Jesus said to them,

"What you have just heard me read has come true today."

All the people started talking about Jesus and were amazed at the wonderful things he said. They kept on asking, "Isn't he Joseph's son?"

Jesus answered:

You will certainly want to tell me this saying, "Doctor, first make yourself well." You will tell me to do the same things here in my own home town that you heard I did in Capernaum. But you can be sure that no prophets are liked by the people of their own home town.

Once during the time of Elijah there was no rain for three and a half years, and people everywhere were starving. There were many widows in Israel, but Elijah was sent only to a widow in the town of Zarephath near the city of Sidon. During the time of the prophet Elisha, many men in Israel had leprosy. But no one was healed, except Naaman who lived in Syria.

When the people in the meeting place heard Jesus say this, they became so angry that they got up and threw him out of town. They dragged him to the edge of the cliff on which the town was built, because they wanted to throw him down from there. But Jesus slipped through the crowd and got away.

A Man with an Evil Spirit

Jesus went to the town of Capernaum in Galilee and taught the people on the Sabbath. His teaching amazed them because he spoke with power. There in the Jewish meeting place was a man with an evil spirit. He yelled out, "Hey, Jesus of Nazareth, what do you want with us? Are you here to get rid of us? I know who you are! You are God's Holy One."

Jesus ordered the evil spirit to be quiet and come out. The demon threw the man to the ground in front of everyone and left without harming him.

They all were amazed and kept saying to each other, "What kind of teaching is this? He has power to order evil spirits out of people!" News about Jesus spread all over that part of the country.

The Judean Desert

> "I read somewhere that this young man, Jesus Christ, went about doing good. But I just go about."
> *Toyohiko Kagawa –*
> *Japanese social reformer*

DID JESUS
REALLY LIVE?

Our main sources of information about Jesus are four written accounts, known as the Gospels. The value of having four separate accounts is that they confirm each other in the overall picture of Jesus' life. In any kind of investigation today, eye-witnesses are asked for their viewpoints, so as to give a clearer picture of what took place. These testimonies differ in the details they record but basically all report the same events and together give a more comprehensive account. So the four Gospels taken together give us a more accurate description of Jesus' words, actions and character.

In addition to the Gospels, several other authors of the time refer to Jesus. Two of them, writing within a century of Jesus' birth, are of particular interest. Flavius Josephus was probably the greatest Jewish historian of his time and certainly no friend of the growing Christian faith. In his book The Antiquities of the Jews he records the following information about Jesus:

"At the time there was a wise man called Jesus. And his conduct was good and he was known to be virtuous. And many people among the Jews and from other nations became his disciples. Pilate condemned him to be crucified and to die. And those who became his disciples did not abandon his discipleship. They reported that he had appeared to them three days later after his crucifixion and that he was alive."

This substantially agrees with the Gospel record. Cornelius Tacitus was a Roman historian who married the daughter of the governor of Britain. In one of his earlier writings, he mentions the execution of Jesus at the order of Pontius Pilate.

Through the writing of the first Christians and other authors from outside the Christian faith we are able to know about the words and life of Jesus. Far from being shaky or uncertain, our knowledge of Jesus is more complete and detailed than for most other figures in the ancient world.

Can we believe the Gospels? See page 22.

See the Evidence pages in the Question and Answer section on www.rejesus.co.uk/the_story

Jesus Heals Many People

Jesus left the meeting place and went to Simon's home. When Jesus got there, he was told that Simon's mother-in-law was sick with a high fever. So Jesus went over to her and ordered the fever to go away. At once she was able to get up and serve them a meal.

After the sun had set, people with all kinds of diseases were brought to Jesus. He put his hands on each one of them and healed them. Demons went out of many people and shouted, "You are the Son of God!" But Jesus ordered the demons not to speak because they knew he was the Messiah.

The next morning Jesus went out to a place where he could be alone, and crowds came looking for him. When they found him, they tried to stop him from leaving. But Jesus said, "People in other towns must hear the good news about God's kingdom. That's why I was sent." So he kept on preaching in the Jewish meeting places in Judea.

Jesus Chooses His First Disciples

Jesus was standing on the shore of Lake Gennesaret, teaching the people as they crowded around him to hear God's message. Near the shore he saw two boats left there by some fishermen who had gone to wash their nets. Jesus got into the boat that belonged to Simon and asked him to row it out a little way from the shore. Then Jesus sat down in the boat to teach the crowd.

When Jesus had finished speaking, he told Simon, "Row the boat out into the deep water and let your nets down to catch some fish."

"Master," Simon answered, "we've worked hard all night long and haven't caught a thing. But if you tell me to, I will let the nets down." They did it and caught so many fish that their nets began ripping apart. Then they signalled for their partners in the other boat to come and help them.

"They left everything and went with Jesus"

The men came, and together they filled the two boats so full that they both began to sink.

When Simon Peter saw this happen, he knelt down in front of Jesus and said, "Lord, don't come near me! I'm a sinner." Peter and everyone with him were completely surprised at all the fish they had caught. His partners James and John, the sons of Zebedee, were surprised too.

Jesus told Simon, "Don't be afraid! From now on you will bring in people instead of fish." The men pulled their boats up on the shore. Then they left everything and went with Jesus.

Jesus Heals a Man with Leprosy

Jesus came to a town where there was a man who had leprosy. When the man saw Jesus, he knelt down to the ground in front of Jesus and begged, "Lord, you have the power to make me well, if only you wanted to."

Jesus put his hand on him and said, "I want to! Now you are well." At once the man's leprosy disappeared. Jesus told him, "Don't tell anyone about this, but go and show yourself to the priest. Offer a gift to the priest, just as Moses commanded, and everyone will know that you have been healed."

News about Jesus kept spreading. Large crowds came to listen to him teach and to be healed of their diseases. But Jesus would often go to a place where he could be alone and pray.

Jesus Heals a Crippled Man

One day some Pharisees and experts in the Law of Moses sat listening to Jesus teach. They had come from every village in Galilee and Judea and from Jerusalem.

God had given Jesus the power to heal the sick, and some people came carrying a crippled man on a mat. They tried to take him inside the house and put him in front of Jesus. But because of the crowd, they couldn't get him to Jesus. So they went up on the roof, where they removed some tiles and let the mat down into the middle of the room.

When Jesus saw how much faith they had, he said to the crippled man, "My friend, your sins are forgiven."

The Pharisees and the experts began arguing, "Jesus must think he is God! Only God can forgive sins."

Boats on Lake Gennesaret (The Sea of Galilee)

* SABBATH

The Sabbath was the seventh day of the Jewish week, on which God intended his people to rest from ordinary work and celebrate his goodness. Of all the Old Testament commandments this had become the most weighed down, with hundreds of interpretations of what work really meant. These were very restrictive and left the people feeling burdened and confused. Sabbath observance became a focus of hot debate between the Pharisees and Jesus.

Cana in Galilee

"Jesus must think he's God!"

Jesus knew what they were thinking, and he said, "Why are you thinking that? Is it easier for me to tell this crippled man that his sins are forgiven or to tell him to get up and walk? But now you will see that the Son of Man has the right to forgive sins here on earth." Jesus then said to the man, "Get up! Pick up your mat and walk home."

At once the man stood up in front of everyone. He picked up his mat and went home, giving thanks to God. Everyone was amazed and praised God. What they saw surprised them, and they said, "We've seen a great miracle today!"

Jesus Chooses Levi

Later, Jesus went out and saw a tax collector named Levi sitting at the place for paying taxes. Jesus said to him, "Come with me." Levi left everything and went with Jesus.

In his home Levi gave a big dinner for Jesus. Many tax collectors and other guests were also there.

The Pharisees and some of their teachers of the Law of Moses grumbled to Jesus' disciples, "Why do you eat and drink with those tax collectors and other sinners?"

Jesus answered, "Healthy people don't need a doctor, but sick people do. I didn't come to invite good people to turn to God. I came to invite sinners."

People Ask about Going without Eating

Some people said to Jesus, "John's followers often pray and go without eating, and so do the followers of the Pharisees. But your disciples never go without eating or drinking."

Jesus told them, "The friends of a bridegroom don't go without eating while he is still with them. But the time will come when he will be taken from them. Then they will go without eating."

Jesus then told them these sayings:

No one uses a new piece of cloth to patch old clothes. The patch would shrink and make the hole even bigger. No one pours new wine into old wineskins. The new wine would swell and burst the old skins. Then the wine would be lost, and the skins would be ruined. New wine must be put only into new wineskins. No one wants new wine after drinking old wine. They say, "The old wine is better."

A Question about the Sabbath

One Sabbath* when Jesus and his disciples were walking through some wheat fields, the disciples picked some wheat. They rubbed the husks off with their hands and started eating the grain.

Some Pharisees said, "Why are you picking grain on the Sabbath? You're not supposed to do that!"

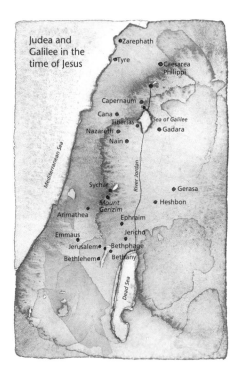

Judea and Galilee in the time of Jesus

Zarephath
Tyre
Caesarea Philippi
Capernaum
Cana
Tiberias
Sea of Galilee
Nazareth
Gadara
Nain
Mediterranean Sea
River Jordan
Sychar
Gerasa
Mount Gerizim
Heshbon
Arimathea
Ephraim
Emmaus
Jericho
Jerusalem
Bethphage
Bethlehem
Bethany
Dead Sea

Jesus answered, "Surely you have read what David did when he and his followers were hungry. He went into the house of God and took the sacred loaves of bread that only priests were supposed to eat. He not only ate some himself, but even gave some to his followers."

Jesus finished by saying, "The Son of Man is Lord over the Sabbath."

A Man with a Crippled Hand

On another Sabbath Jesus was teaching in a Jewish meeting place, and a man with a crippled right hand was there. Some Pharisees and teachers of the Law of Moses kept watching Jesus to see if he would heal the man. They did this because they wanted to accuse Jesus of doing something wrong.

Jesus knew what they were thinking. So he told the man to stand up where everyone could see him. And the man stood up. Then Jesus asked, "On the Sabbath should we do good deeds or evil deeds? Should we save someone's life or destroy it?"

After he had looked around at everyone, he told the man, "Stretch out your hand." He did, and his bad hand became completely well.

The teachers and the Pharisees were furious and started saying to each other, "What can we do about Jesus?"

Life Story

DEBBIE MENELAWS

"I am proof of the power of God. I owe him everything."

Debbie Menelaws was brought up in a family steeped in occult practices. As she grew up she got more and more deeply involved in astrology.

"I read fortunes, including tarot card and palm reading and I used the psychic powers I had to participate as a medium in seances. I thought I knew God. I believed myself to be a very spiritual person and was seeking power to help other people. Unfortunately the results of my occult involvement left me suffering from depression. I had a very deep emptiness and unhappiness in my life."

"Then someone came and told me about Jesus. Nobody had told me before that Jesus was the only way to reach God. I immediately experienced a deep sense of sin in my life, but Jesus showed me his love. He cleansed me and I knew I was forgiven. Jesus came and filled all the empty places and I was emotionally healed and delivered. My whole family came to the Lord. I now know that God is my heavenly Father and that I have the power of his Holy Spirit working in my life."

NEW THINKING

About that time Jesus went off to a mountain to pray, and he spent the whole night there. The next morning he called his disciples together and chose twelve of them to be his apostles.

One was Simon, and Jesus named him Peter. Another was Andrew, Peter's brother. There were also James, John, Philip, Bartholomew, Matthew, Thomas, and James the son of Alphaeus. The rest of the apostles were Simon, known as the Eager One, Jude, who was the son of James, and Judas Iscariot, who later betrayed Jesus.

Jesus Teaches, Preaches, and Heals

Jesus and his apostles went down from the mountain and came to some flat, level ground. Many other disciples were there to meet him. Large crowds of people from all over Judea, Jerusalem, and the coastal cities of Tyre and Sidon were there too. These people had come to listen to Jesus and to be healed of their diseases. All who were troubled by evil spirits were also healed. Everyone was trying to touch Jesus, because power was going out from him and healing them all.

Blessings and Troubles

Jesus looked at his disciples and said:

God will bless you people who are poor.
His kingdom belongs to you!
God will bless
you hungry people.
You will have plenty
to eat!
God will bless you people who are crying.
You will laugh!
God will bless you when others hate you and won't have anything to do with

you. God will bless you when people insult you and say cruel things about you, all because you are a follower of the Son of Man. Long ago your own people did these same things to the prophets. So when this happens to you, be happy and jump for joy! You will have a great reward in heaven.

But you rich people are in for trouble. You have already had an easy life! You well-fed people are in for trouble. You will go hungry! You people who are laughing now are in for trouble. You are going to cry and weep!

You are in for trouble when everyone says good things about you. That's what your own people said about those prophets who told lies.

Love for Enemies
This is what I say to all who will listen to me:

Love your enemies, and be good to everyone who hates you. Ask God to bless anyone who curses you, and pray for everyone who is cruel to you. If someone slaps you on one cheek, don't stop that person from slapping you on the other cheek. If someone wants to take your coat, don't try to keep back your shirt. Give to everyone who asks and don't ask people to return what they have taken from you. Treat others just as you want to be treated.

If you love only someone who loves you, will God praise you for that? Even sinners love people who love them. If you are kind only to someone who is kind to you, will God be pleased with you for that? Even sinners are kind

> ## "Forgive others, and God will forgive you"

to people who are kind to them. If you lend money only to someone you think will pay you back, will God be pleased with you for that? Even sinners lend to sinners because they think they will get it all back.

But love your enemies and be good to them. Lend without expecting to be paid back. Then you will get a great reward, and you will be the true children of God in heaven. He is good even to people who are unthankful and cruel. Have pity on others, just as your Father has pity on you.

Judging Others
Jesus said:

Don't judge others, and God won't judge you. Don't be hard on others, and God won't be hard on you.

Forgive others, and God will forgive you. If you give to others, you will be given a full amount in return. It will be packed down, shaken together, and spilling over into your lap. The way you treat others is the way you will be treated.

Jesus also used some sayings as he spoke to the people. He said:

Can one blind person lead another blind person? Won't they both fall into a ditch? Are students better than

> ## "The things that most people think are important are worthless as far as God is concerned."
> *Jesus*

Stressed out by life?
See www.rejesus.co.uk/stress

What is love?
See www.rejesus.co.uk/love

CAN WE BELIEVE THE GOSPELS?

The Gospels claim to be based on eye-witness accounts of the events in Jesus' life. This raises two questions. Firstly, how close to the events they claim to record were the original gospels written? Secondly, given that we do not have the original documents, how reliable are the copies that exist today?

Research this century has confirmed that the Gospels by Matthew, Mark and Luke were likely to have been written within 30 or 40 years of the events they record. People still remembered Jesus very clearly at this time and would not have swallowed a lot of exaggerated claims.

There are over 24,000 existing manuscripts which contain the whole or part of the New Testament and a number were copied very near to the time of the events they describe.

This contrasts with Caesar's 'Gallic Wars', for example, for which the oldest copy surviving today was made over 900 years after the original was written. This is typical of ancient manuscripts. In fact, the manuscript evidence for the Gospels and the rest of the New Testament is far more plentiful than for any other ancient book. Because of the wealth of the evidence and its early date, modern scholars have no doubts about the basic reliability of the transmission of the New Testament documents. In this way we can check the accuracy of the text of our modern translations and see that it has remained unchanged through history.

Who did Jesus claim to be?
See page 30.

See the Evidence pages in the Question and Answer section on www.rejesus.co.uk/the_story

NEW TESTAMENT

AUTHOR'S WRITING → **40 YEARS** → OLDEST SURVIVING FRAGMENTS OF COPY

GALLIC WARS BY JULIUS CAESAR

AUTHOR'S WRITING → **900 YEARS** – – – → OLDEST SURVIVING COPY

their teacher? But when they are fully trained, they will be like their teacher.

You can see the speck in your friend's eye. But you don't notice the log in your own eye. How can you say, "My friend, let me take the

"Your words show what is in your heart"

speck out of your eye," when you don't see the log in your own eye? You show-offs! First, get the log out of your own eye. Then you can see how to take the speck out of your friend's eye.

A Tree and Its Fruit
A good tree can't produce bad fruit, and a bad tree can't produce good fruit. You can tell what a tree is like by the fruit it produces. You can't pick figs or grapes from thorn bushes. Good people do good things because of the good in their hearts. Bad people do bad things because of the evil in their hearts. Your words show what is in your heart.

Two Builders
Why do you keep on saying that I am your Lord, when you refuse to do what I say? Anyone who comes and listens to me and obeys me is like someone who dug down deep and built a house on solid rock. When the flood came and the river rushed against the house, it was built so well that it didn't even shake. But anyone who hears what I say and doesn't

obey me is like someone whose house wasn't built on solid rock. As soon as the river rushed against that house, it was smashed to pieces!

Jesus Heals an Army Officer's Servant

After Jesus had finished teaching the people, he went to Capernaum. In that town an army officer's servant was sick and about to die. The officer liked this servant very much. And when he heard about Jesus, he sent some Jewish leaders to ask him to come and heal the servant.

The leaders went to Jesus and begged him to do something. They said, "This man deserves your help! He loves our nation and even built us a meeting place." So Jesus went with them.

When Jesus wasn't far from the house, the officer sent some friends to tell him, "Lord, don't go to any trouble for me! I'm not good enough for you to come into my house. And I'm certainly not worthy to come to you.

Just say the word, and my servant will get well. I have officers who give orders to me, and I have soldiers who take orders from me. I can say to one of them, 'Go!' and he goes. I can say to another, 'Come!' and he comes. I can say to my servant, 'Do this!' and he'll do it."

When Jesus heard this, he was so surprised that he turned and said to the crowd following him, "In all of Israel I've never found anyone with this much faith!"

The officer's friends

returned and found the servant well.

A Widow's Son

Soon Jesus and his disciples were on their way to the town of Nain, and a big crowd was going along with them. As they came near the gate of the town, they saw people carrying out the body of a widow's only son. Many people from the town were walking along with her.

When the Lord saw the woman, he felt sorry for her and said, "Don't cry!"

Jesus went over and touched the stretcher on which the people were carrying the dead boy. They stopped, and Jesus said, "Young man, get up!" The boy sat up and began to speak. Jesus then gave him back to his mother.

Everyone was frightened and praised God. They said, "A great prophet is here with us! God has come to his people."

News about Jesus spread all over Judea and everywhere else in that part of the country.

John the Baptist

John's followers told John everything that was being said about Jesus. So he sent two of them to ask the Lord, "Are you the one we should be looking for? Or must we wait for someone else?"

When these messengers came to Jesus, they said, "John the Baptist sent us to ask, 'Are you the one we should be looking for? Or are we supposed to wait for someone else?'"

At that time Jesus was healing many people who were sick or in pain or were troubled by evil spirits, and he was giving sight to a lot of blind people. Jesus said to the messengers sent by John, "Go and tell John what you have seen and heard. Blind people are now able to see, and the lame can walk. People who have leprosy are being healed, and the deaf can now hear. The dead are raised to life, and the poor are hearing the good news. God will bless everyone who doesn't reject me because of what I do."

After John's messengers had gone, Jesus began speaking to the crowds about John:

What kind of person did you go out to the desert to see? Was he like tall grass blown about by the wind? What kind of man did you really go out to see? Was he someone dressed in fine clothes?

People who wear expensive clothes and live in luxury

> "Men occasionally stumble over the truth, but most of them pick themselves up and hurry off as if nothing happened."
> *Winston Churchill*

A town in Galilee

> "The biggest disease today is not leprosy or tuberculosis but rather a feeling of being unwanted, uncared for and deserted by everybody. The greatest evil is the lack of love and charity."
>
> *Mother Teresa*

are in the king's palace. What then did you go out to see? Was he a prophet? He certainly was! I tell you that he was more than a prophet. In the Scriptures, God calls John his messenger and says, "I'm sending my messenger ahead of you to get things ready for you." No one ever born on this earth is greater than John. But whoever is least important in God's kingdom is greater than John.

Everyone had been listening to John. Even the tax collectors had obeyed God and had done what was right by letting John baptise them. But the Pharisees and the experts in the Law of Moses refused to obey God and be baptised by John.

Jesus went on to say:
What are you people like? What kind of people are you? You are like children sitting in the market and shouting to

each other,
"We played the flute, but you wouldn't dance! We sang a funeral song, but you wouldn't cry!"
John the Baptist didn't go around eating and drinking, and you said, "John has a demon in him!" But because the Son of Man goes around eating and drinking, you say, "Jesus eats and drinks too much! He is even a friend of tax collectors and sinners." Yet Wisdom is shown to be right by what its followers do.

Simon the Pharisee

A Pharisee invited Jesus to have dinner with him. So Jesus went to the Pharisee's home and got ready to eat.

When a sinful woman in that town found out that Jesus was there, she bought an expensive bottle of perfume. Then she came and stood behind Jesus. She cried and started washing his feet with her tears and drying them with her hair. The woman kissed his feet and poured the perfume on them.

The Pharisee who had invited Jesus saw this and said to himself, "If this man really was a prophet, he would know what kind of woman is touching him! He would know that she is a sinner."

Jesus said to the Pharisee, "Simon, I have something to say to you."

"Teacher, what is it?" Simon replied.

Jesus told him, "Two people were in debt to a moneylender. One of them owed him 500 silver coins, and the other owed

him 50. Since neither of them could pay him back, the moneylender said that they didn't have to pay him anything. Which one of them will like him more?"

Simon answered, "I suppose it would be the one who had owed more and didn't have to pay it back."

"You are right," Jesus said.

He turned towards the woman and said to Simon, "Have you noticed this woman? When I came into your home, you didn't give me any water so I could wash my feet. But she has washed my feet with her tears and dried them with her hair. You didn't greet me with a kiss, but from the time I came in, she has not stopped kissing

"Your sins are forgiven"

my feet. You didn't even pour olive oil on my head, but she has poured expensive perfume on my feet. So I tell you that all her sins are forgiven, and that is why she has shown great love. But anyone who has been forgiven for only a little will show only a little love."

Then Jesus said to the woman, "Your sins are forgiven."

Some other guests started saying to one another, "Who is this who dares to forgive sins?"

But Jesus told the woman, "Because of your faith, you are now saved. May God give you peace!"

Life Story

HAMISH MACGREGOR

"It seems that this healing was God's way of getting my attention."

A football injury, followed by a serious back injury whilst weight training left Hamish MacGregor in severe pain and unable to go to work. Movement was very hard and very slow. During this time he was invited to attend a church service. Here he met people who were lively and seemed to enjoy church. After the talk on this particular occasion, the speaker offered to pray for anyone who asked.

"This was new to me, so I sat to observe the outcome of those who were prayed for. My friend George, along with my wife, decided to encourage me to ask for prayer. I was resistant for a while but finally agreed."

"When I was asked if I believed that Jesus could heal me I didn't know what to say. My friend George, who had helped me walk slowly and painfully to the front, told me to say yes. The preacher then asked Jesus to heal me. I experienced a surge of some kind of power that came down upon my head and engulfed me

completely. There was no fear attached to this – in fact it was quite pleasant. With my eyes closed, I saw a window with a blind pulled down creating pitch darkness. Suddenly the blind shot up and light flooded in. The moment this happened my back was healed. The whole episode lasted only a few minutes."

"I had no more trouble with that injury again."

"Because of what happened I began to look more seriously at who Jesus Christ is. Within a few weeks of my healing, I had come to appreciate that Christ died for me and rose again from the dead. Both my wife and I started to let Christ take control of our lives. That healing took place over thirteen years ago and was just the beginning of what God was about to do with my life. Coming to know him has been the best thing that has happened to me."

WORD GETS AROUND

One of the women was Mary Magdalene, who once had seven demons in her. Joanna, Susanna, and many others had also used what they owned to help Jesus and his disciples. Joanna's husband Chuza was one of Herod's officials.

A Story about a Farmer

When a large crowd from several towns had gathered around Jesus, he told them this story:

A farmer went out to scatter seed in a field. While the farmer was doing it, some of the seeds fell along the road and were stepped on or eaten by birds. Other seeds fell on rocky ground and started growing. But the plants didn't have enough water and soon dried up. Some other seeds fell where thorn bushes grew up and choked the plants. The rest of the seeds fell on good ground where they grew and produced 100 times as many seeds.

When Jesus had finished speaking, he said, "If you have ears, pay attention!"

Soon after this, Jesus was going through towns and villages, telling the good news about God's kingdom*. His twelve apostles were with him, and so were some women who had been healed of evil spirits and all sorts of diseases.

Why Jesus Used Stories

Jesus' disciples asked him what the story meant. So he answered:

I have explained the secrets about God's kingdom* to you, but for others I can only use stories. These people look, but they don't see, and they hear, but they don't understand.

Jesus Explains the Story about the Farmer

This is what the story means: The seed is God's message, and the seeds that fell along the road are the people who hear the message. But the devil comes and snatches the message out of their hearts, so that they won't believe and be saved. The seeds that fell on rocky ground are the people who gladly hear the message and accept it. But they don't have deep roots, and they believe only for a little while. As soon as life gets hard, they give up.

The seeds that fell among the thorn bushes are also people who hear the message. But they are so eager for riches and pleasures that they never produce anything. Those seeds that fell on good ground are the people who listen to the message and keep it in good and honest hearts. They last and produce a harvest.

Light

No one lights a lamp and puts it under a bowl or under a bed. A lamp is always put on a lampstand, so that people who come into a house will see the light. There is nothing hidden that won't be found.

There is no secret that won't be well known. Pay attention to how you listen! Everyone who has something will be given more, but people who have nothing will lose what little they think they have.

Jesus' Mother and Brothers

Jesus' mother and brothers went to see him, but because of the crowd they couldn't get near him. Someone told Jesus, "Your mother and brothers are standing outside and want to see you."

Jesus answered, "My mother and my brothers are those people who hear and obey God's message."

A Storm

One day, Jesus and his disciples got into a boat, and he said, "Let's cross the lake." They started out, and while they were sailing across, he went to sleep.

Suddenly a strong wind struck the lake, and the boat started sinking. They were in danger. So they went to Jesus and woke him up, "Master, Master! We're about to drown!"

Jesus got up and ordered the wind and waves to stop.

"Who is this?"

They obeyed, and everything was calm. Then Jesus asked the disciples, "Don't you have any faith?"

But they were frightened and amazed. They said to each other, "Who is this? He can give orders to the wind and the waves, and they obey him!"

27

* DEMONS

Demons, evil spirits or unclean spirits are hardly mentioned in the New Testament outside the gospel accounts of Jesus' life. The very presence of Jesus provoked unprecedented hostility from the devil and the forces of evil. The most convincing evidence for belief in the devil is that Jesus took Satan's reality seriously, speaking of him as an evil prince who ruled the world. Jesus saw his miracles as part of the process of driving back his opponent's kingdom and spoke of his own death as the final victory to break the devil's rule.

A Man with Demons in Him

Jesus and his disciples sailed across Lake Galilee and came to shore near the town of Gerasa. As Jesus was getting out of the boat, he was met by a man from that town. The man had demons* in him. He had gone naked for a long time and no longer lived in a house, but in the graveyard.

The man saw Jesus and screamed. He knelt down in front of him and shouted, "Jesus, Son of God in heaven, what do you want with me? I beg you not to torture me!" He said this because Jesus had already told the evil spirit to go out of him.

The man had often been attacked by the demon. And even though he had been bound with chains and leg irons and kept under guard, he smashed whatever bound him. Then the demon would force him out into lonely places.

Jesus asked the man, "What's your name?"

He answered, "My name is Lots." He said this because there were 'lots' of demons in him. They begged Jesus not to send them to the deep pit, where they would be punished.

A large herd of pigs was feeding there on the hillside. So the demons begged Jesus to let them go into the pigs, and Jesus let them go. Then the demons left the man and went into the pigs. The whole herd rushed down the steep bank into the lake and drowned.

When the men taking care of the pigs saw this, they ran to spread the news in the town and on the farms. The people went out to see what had happened, and when they came to Jesus, they also found the man. The demons had gone out of him, and he was sitting there at the feet of Jesus. He had clothes on and was in his right mind. But the people were terrified.

Then all who had seen the man healed talked about it. Everyone from around Gerasa begged Jesus to leave, because they were so frightened.

When Jesus got into the boat to start back, the man who had been healed begged to go with him. But Jesus sent him off and said, "Go back home and tell everyone how much God has done for you." The man then went all over town, telling everything that Jesus had done for him.

A Dying Girl and a Sick Woman

Everyone had been waiting for Jesus, and when he came back, a crowd was there to welcome him. Just then the man in charge of the Jewish meeting place came and knelt down in front of Jesus. His name was Jairus, and he begged Jesus to come to his home because his 12-year-old child was dying. She was his only daughter.

While Jesus was on his way, people were crowding all around him. In the crowd was a woman who had been bleeding for years. She had spent everything she had on doctors, but none of them could make her well.

As soon as she came up behind Jesus and barely touched his clothes, her bleeding stopped.

"Who touched me?" Jesus asked.

While everyone was denying it, Peter said, "Master, people are crowding all around and pushing you from every side."

But Jesus answered, "Someone touched me, because I felt power going out from me." The woman knew that she couldn't hide, so she came trembling and knelt down in front of Jesus. She told everyone why she had touched him and that she had been healed straight away.

Jesus said to the woman, "You're now well because of your faith. May God give you peace!"

While Jesus was speaking, someone came from Jairus' home and said, "Your

Life Story

GRAHAM FINDLAY

When Graham Findlay came to Edinburgh, he was a heroin addict. He had used drugs for four years.

His mother had been praying for him for quite some time. There was about to be a powerful and dramatic answer.

"I was seven and a half stone and near death. I sought help from Bethany Christian Centre. It was my last hope. When I came I didn't expect anything to change but I was wrong. In the past I had heard people tell me of God's love, but at the Centre I wasn't just told of God's love, I was shown it. I realised then that I needed to be saved. I prayed and handed my life over to Jesus."

"I woke up the following morning to discover God had immediately healed me from my addiction. I have been drug free since February 1992 and am now eleven stone. I really love Jesus and am so thankful to him for the change in my life. Things aren't always easy and sometimes it's tough; but that's life! I'm reminded of the words of Jesus, 'In this world you will have trouble, but take heart, I have overcome the world'. With Jesus we can overcome all things."

Graham now works at Bethany Christian Centre himself, helping others to come off drugs. He is married. He loves telling others what God has done for him, showing love to those with whom he is in contact.

WHO DID JESUS CLAIM TO BE?

"Do you want to know what God is like? Look at me!" (John 14:9) "I am the only person who can lead you to God" (John 14:6). Jesus claimed to speak for God and do the things that only God could do, such as forgiving sin. Inspite of that, many people like to think of him just as a great religious teacher, the founder of one of the world religions. They see him on the same sort of level as the Buddha or Mohammed. However, what Jesus said about himself finds no equivalent in any of the other world religions. In fact, quite the opposite.

Buddha directed attention away from himself, so that his disciples would not be distracted in their search for release from earthly sensations and pleasures. He did not see himself or any other teacher as essential to this search.

Mohammed, the founder of Islam, also pointed away from himself. Very little is said about him in the Quran. He insisted that he was only a man, without any supernatural powers beyond receiving the Quran from the hands of Allah.

Jesus was very different from these two religious figures. He had a great deal to say about himself. Muslim and Buddhist beliefs rest on the teaching of Mohammed and Buddha. Christian belief centres on the person of Jesus.

No-one in their right mind would dream of saying the things Jesus said about himself, unless they were true. Of course, you might think that Jesus was mad, or a confidence trickster. But when we look at the way Jesus lived, his compassion for those on the fringes of society and the quality and wisdom of his teaching, it is difficult to come to the conclusion that he was evil or insane.

Wasn't Jesus just a good man?
See page 40.

See the Identity pages in the Question and Answer section on www.rejesus.co.uk/the_story

daughter has died! Why bother the teacher anymore?"

When Jesus heard this, he told Jairus, "Don't worry! Have faith, and your daughter will get well."

Jesus went into the house, but he didn't let anyone else go with him, except Peter, John, James, and the girl's father and mother. Everyone was crying and weeping for the girl. But Jesus said, "The child isn't dead. She is just asleep." The people laughed at him because they knew she was dead.

Jesus took hold of the girl's hand and said, "Child, get up!" She came back to life and got straight up. Jesus told them to give her something to eat. Her parents were surprised, but Jesus ordered them not to tell anyone what had happened.

Instructions for the Twelve Apostles

Jesus called together his twelve apostles and gave them complete power over all demons and diseases. Then he sent them to tell everyone about God's kingdom and to heal the sick. He told them, "Don't take anything with you! Don't take a walking stick or a travelling bag or food or money or even a change of clothes. When you are welcomed into a home, stay there until you leave that town. If people won't welcome you, leave the town and shake the dust from your feet as a warning to them."

The apostles left and went from village to village, telling the good news and healing people everywhere.

Herod Is Worried

Herod the ruler heard about all that was happening, and he was worried. Some people were saying that John the Baptist had come back to life. Others were saying that Elijah had come or that one of the prophets from long ago had come back to life. But Herod said, "I had John's head cut off! Who is this I hear so much about?" Herod was eager to meet Jesus.

Jesus Feeds 5000

The apostles came back and told Jesus everything they had done. He then took them with him to the village of Bethsaida, where they could be alone. But a lot of people found out about this and followed him. Jesus welcomed them. He spoke to them about God's kingdom and healed everyone who was sick.

Late in the afternoon the twelve apostles came to Jesus and said, "Send the crowd to the villages and farms around here. They need to find a place to stay and something to eat. There is nothing in this place. It's like a desert!"

Jesus answered, "You give them something to eat."

But they replied, "We've only got five small loaves of bread and two fish. If we are going to feed all these people, we will have to go and buy food." There were about 5000 men in the crowd.

Jesus said to his disciples, "Tell the people to sit in groups of 50." They did this, and all the people sat down. Jesus took the five loaves and the two fish. He looked up towards heaven and blessed the food. Then he broke the bread and fish and handed them to his disciples to give to the people.

Everyone ate all they wanted. What was left over filled 12 baskets.

"Christianity will go. We're more popular than Jesus now."
John Lennon

Who Is Jesus?

When Jesus was alone praying, his disciples came to him, and he asked them, "What do people say about me?"

They answered, "Some say that you are John the Baptist or Elijah or a prophet from long ago who has come back to life."

"Who do you say I am?"

Jesus then asked them, "But who do you say I am?"

Peter answered, "You are the Messiah sent from God."

Jesus strictly warned his disciples not to tell anyone about this.

Jesus Speaks about His Suffering and Death

Jesus told his disciples, "The nation's leaders, the chief priests, and the teachers of the Law of Moses will make the Son of Man* suffer terribly. They will reject him and kill him, but three days later he will rise to life."

Then Jesus said to all the people:

If any of you want to be my followers, you must forget about yourself. You must take up your cross each day and follow me. If you want to save your life, you will destroy it. But if you give up your life for me, you will save it. What will you gain, if you own the whole world but destroy yourself or waste your life? If you are ashamed of me and my message, the Son of Man will be ashamed of you when he comes in his glory and in the glory of his Father and the holy angels. You can be sure that some of the people standing here won't die before they see God's kingdom.

The True Glory of Jesus

About eight days later Jesus took Peter, John, and James with him and went up on a mountain to pray. While he was praying, his face changed, and his clothes became shining white. Suddenly Moses and Elijah were there speaking with him. They appeared in heavenly glory and talked about all that Jesus' death in Jerusalem would mean.

Peter and the other two disciples had been sound asleep. All at once they woke up and saw how glorious Jesus was. They also saw the two men who were with him.

Moses and Elijah were about to leave, when Peter said to Jesus, "Master, it's good for us to be here! Let's make three shelters, one for you, one for Moses, and one for Elijah." But Peter didn't know what he was talking about.

While Peter was still speaking, a shadow from a cloud passed over them, and they were frightened as the cloud covered them. From the cloud a voice spoke, "This is my chosen Son. Listen to what he says!"

After the voice had spoken, Peter, John, and James saw only Jesus. For some time they kept quiet and didn't say anything about what they had seen.

Jesus Heals a Boy
The next day Jesus and his three disciples came down from the mountain and were met by a large crowd. Just then someone in the crowd shouted, "Teacher, please do something for my son! He's my only child! A demon often attacks him and makes him scream. It shakes him until he foams at the mouth, and it won't leave him until it has completely worn the boy out. I begged your disciples to force out the demon, but they couldn't do it."

Jesus said to them, "You people are stubborn and don't have any faith!

How much longer must I be with you? Why do I have to put up with you?"

Then Jesus said to the man, "Bring your son to me." While the boy was being brought, the demon attacked him and made him shake all over. Jesus ordered the demon to stop. Then he healed the boy and gave him back to his father. Everyone was amazed at God's great power.

Jesus Again Speaks about His Death
While everyone was still amazed at what Jesus was doing, he said to his disciples, "Pay close attention to what I'm telling you! The Son of Man* will be handed over to his enemies." But the disciples didn't know what he meant. The meaning was hidden from them. They couldn't understand it, and they were afraid to ask.

Who Is the Greatest?
Jesus' disciples were arguing about which one of them was the greatest. Jesus knew what they were thinking, and he had a child stand there beside him. Then he said to his disciples, "When you welcome even a child because of me, you welcome me. And when you welcome me, you welcome the one who sent me. Whichever one of you is the most humble is the greatest."

For or Against Jesus
John said, "Master, we saw a man using your name to force demons out of people. But we told him to stop, because he isn't one of us."

"Don't stop him!" Jesus said. "Anyone who isn't against you is for you."

* SON OF MAN
Jesus often referred to himself as the Son of Man – another title for the Messiah in the Old Testament. The title was not obviously understood, making it possible for him to invest it with his own meaning. He used it many times. It emphasises his identification with humanity and he often linked it with his suffering and death.

NO TURNING BACK

Not long before it was time for Jesus to be taken up to heaven, he made up his mind to go to Jerusalem. He sent some messengers on ahead to a Samaritan village to get things ready for him. But he was on his way to Jerusalem, so the people there refused to welcome him.

When the disciples James and John saw what was happening, they asked, "Lord, do you want us to call down fire from heaven to destroy these people?"

But Jesus turned and corrected them for what they had said. Then they all went on to another village.

Three People Who Wanted To Be Followers

Along the way someone said to Jesus, "I'll go anywhere with you!"

Jesus said, "Foxes have dens, and birds have nests, but the Son of Man doesn't have a place to call his own."

Jesus told someone else to come with him. But the man said, "Lord, let me wait until I bury my father."

Jesus answered, "Let the dead take care of the dead, while you go and tell others about God's kingdom."

Then someone said to Jesus, "I want to go with you, Lord, but first let me go back and take care of things at home."

Jesus answered, "Anyone who starts ploughing and keeps looking back isn't worth anything to God's kingdom!"

The Work of the 72 Followers

Later the Lord chose 72 other followers and sent them out two by two to every town and village where he was about to go. He said to them:

A large crop is in the fields, but there are only a few workers. Ask the Lord in charge of the harvest to send out workers to bring it

in. Now go, but remember, I am sending you like lambs into a pack of wolves. Don't take along a moneybag or a travelling bag or sandals. And don't waste time greeting people on the road. As soon as you enter a home, say, "God bless this home with peace." If the people living there are peace-loving, your prayer for peace will bless them. But if they are not peace-loving, your prayer will return to you. Stay with the same family, eating and drinking whatever they give you, because workers are worth what they earn. Don't move around from house to house.

If the people of a town welcome you, eat whatever they offer. Heal their sick and say, "God's kingdom will soon be here!"

But if the people of a town refuse to welcome you, go out into the street and say, "We are shaking the dust from our feet as a warning to you. And you can be sure that God's kingdom will soon be here!" I tell you that on the day of judgment the people of Sodom will get off easier than the people of that town!

The Unbelieving Towns

You people of Chorazin are in for trouble! You people of Bethsaida are also in for trouble! If the miracles that took place in your towns had happened in Tyre and Sidon, the people there would have turned to God long ago. They would have dressed in sackcloth and put ashes on their heads. On the day

"Anyone who says "No" to me is really saying "No" to the one who sent me"

of judgment the people of Tyre and Sidon will get off easier than you will. People of Capernaum, do you think you will be honoured in heaven? Well, you will go down to hell!

My followers, whoever listens to you is listening to me. Anyone who says "No" to you is saying "No" to me.

And anyone who says "No" to me is really saying "No" to the one who sent me.

The Return of the 72

When the 72 followers returned, they were excited and said, "Lord, even the demons obeyed when we spoke in your name!"
Jesus told them:

I saw Satan fall from

heaven like a flash of lightning. I have given you the power to trample on snakes and scorpions and to defeat the power of your enemy Satan. Nothing can harm you. But don't be happy because evil spirits obey you. Be happy that your names are written in heaven!

"The Christian ideal has not been tried and found wanting. It has been found difficult, and left untried."
G K Chesterton

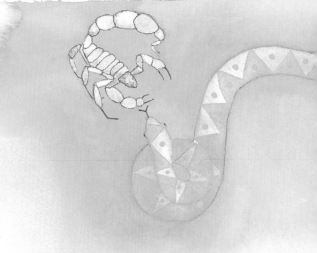

Life Story

MARK BYRON

Our marriage at one point was on a knife-edge of breaking down. Now God has rescued it and made it stronger than ever before.

For the first 14 years of their married life Mark and his wife lived only for themselves. Then a number of things happened that put pressure on that life. Mark's father and business partner died suddenly, followed a year later by the death of his brother-in-law and work colleague. Under the extra work pressure, Mark's drinking habit changed from sociable to alcoholic. Before long he and Karen found themselves living together and yet in two separate lives.

"Just as our lives reached a destructive point, we discovered Karen had become pregnant. For 14 years we had decided to live for ourselves and not have children, so this was somewhat of a shock."

"When Emily was 1 year old we decided to have her christened, as it seemed the thing to do. Looking back, I can see this was when God started revealing himself to us. The first time we attended the local church we felt a love neither of us could explain."

"Karen attended a course to find out more about Christian faith. I said I was too busy to go. But I started to read the Bible out of curiosity and became fascinated by the people whom God revealed himself to and yet who kept turning their backs on him. Eventually I became hooked by the person of Jesus. When he took away my craving for alcohol, I realised that Jesus really is alive and active on this earth."

"As Karen and I have learnt more of God's purpose for our lives our outlook has changed. The pursuit of our own wants has gone and the need to share and care for each other and those around us has grown. We have learned to love each other in a new way – God's way. As a couple who never wanted children, we now have two of our own. And, to top it all, God has led us to become foster carers."

Jesus Thanks his Father

At that same time, Jesus felt the joy that comes from the Holy Spirit, and he said:

My Father, Lord of heaven and earth, I am grateful that you hid all this from wise and educated people and showed it to ordinary people. Yes, Father, that is what pleased you.

My Father has given me everything, and he is the only one who knows the Son. The only one who really knows the Father is the Son. But the Son wants to tell others about the Father, so that they can know him too.

Jesus then turned to his disciples and said to them in private, "You are really blessed to see what you see! Many prophets and kings were eager to see what you see and to hear what you hear. But I tell you that they didn't see or hear."

The Good Samaritan*

An expert in the Law of Moses stood up and asked Jesus a question to see what he would say. "Teacher," he asked, "what must I do to have eternal life?"

Jesus answered, "What is written in the Scriptures? How do you understand them?"

The man replied, "The Scriptures say, 'Love the Lord your God with all your heart, soul, strength, and mind.' They also say, 'Love your neighbours as much as you love yourself.'"

Jesus said, "You have given the right answer. If you do this, you will have eternal life."

But the man wanted to show that he knew what he was talking about. So he asked Jesus, "Who are my neighbours?"

Jesus replied:

As a man was going down from Jerusalem to Jericho, robbers attacked him and grabbed everything he had. They beat him up and ran off, leaving him half dead.

A priest happened to be going down the same road. But when he saw the man, he walked by on the other side. Later a temple helper came to the same place. But when he saw the man who had been beaten up, he also went by on the other side.

A man from Samaria then came travelling along that road. When he saw the man, he felt sorry for him and went over to him. He treated his wounds with olive oil and wine and bandaged them. Then he put him on his own donkey and took him to an inn, where he took care of him. The next morning he gave the innkeeper two silver coins and said, "Please take care of the man. If you spend more than this on him, I will pay you when I return."

Then Jesus asked, "Which one of these three people was a real neighbour to the man who was beaten up by robbers?"

The teacher answered, "The one who showed pity."

Jesus said, "Go and do the same!"

* SAMARITAN

The Samaritans came from the region between Judea and Galilee. Over the years they had intermarried with other races and in Jesus' time were only part-Jewish. They had different customs and sacred places and worshipped God in ways unacceptable to the Jews. This caused the Jews to feel superior and led to hatred between the two groups. It was almost impossible for a Jew to think of people from Samaria as 'good' or worthy of personal contact.

Post your own prayer online at www.rejesus.co.uk/spirituality

Martha and Mary

The Lord and his disciples were travelling along and came to a village. When they got there, a woman named Martha welcomed him into her home. She had a sister named Mary, who sat down in front of the Lord and was listening to what he said. Martha was worried about all that had to be done. Finally, she went to Jesus and said, "Lord, doesn't it bother you that my sister has left me to do all the work by myself? Tell her to come and help me!"

The Lord answered, "Martha, Martha! You are worried and upset about so many things, but only one thing is necessary. Mary has chosen what is best, and it won't be taken away from her."

Prayer

When Jesus had finished praying, one of his disciples said to him, "Lord, teach us to pray, just as John taught his followers to pray."

So Jesus told them, "Pray in this way:

'Father, help us
to honour your name.
Come and set up
your kingdom.
Give us each day
the food we need.
Forgive our sins,
as we forgive everyone
who has done wrong to us.
And keep us
from being tempted.'"

Then Jesus went on to say:

Suppose one of you goes to a friend in the middle of the night and says, "Let me borrow three loaves of bread. A friend of mine has dropped in, and I haven't got anything for him to eat." And suppose your friend answers, "Don't bother me! The door is bolted, and my children and I are in bed. I can't get up to give you anything."

He may not get up and give you the bread, just because you are his friend. But he will get up and give you as much as you need, simply because you aren't ashamed to keep on asking.

So I tell you to ask and you will receive, search and you will find, knock and the door will be opened for you. Everyone who asks will receive, everyone who searches will find, and the door will be opened for everyone who knocks. Which one of you fathers would give your hungry child a snake if the child asked for a fish? Which one of you would give your child a scorpion if the child asked for an egg? As bad as you are, you still know how to give good gifts to your children. But your heavenly Father is even more ready to give the Holy Spirit to anyone who asks.

Jesus and the Ruler of Demons

Jesus forced a demon out of a man who couldn't talk. And after the demon had gone out, the man started speaking, and the crowds were amazed. But some people said, "He forces out demons by the power of Beelzebul, the ruler of the demons!"

Others wanted to put Jesus to the test. So they asked him to show them a sign from God. Jesus knew what they were thinking, and he said:

A kingdom where people fight each other will end up lin ruin. And a family that fights will break up. If Satan fights against himself, how can his kingdom last? Yet you say that I force out demons by the power of Beelzebul. If I use his power to force out demons, whose power do

Life Story

JOHN & HEATHER TOMSON

"We used to be quite selfish, but now our values and priorities have changed."

For many years John & Heather Tomson never gave the Christian faith much thought.

"After Heather and I married, we always went regularly to church – once a year, on Christmas Eve! When our first son came along, we decided to have him christened, but perhaps for the wrong reasons. He was about 18 months old when we thought we ought to do something about the promises we'd made at the christening. As a result, we started going to the church in our village."

"It's only in the last ten years that I'd say we have become everyday Christians instead of just Sunday Christians. Through the people we met at church and the things we heard there, we learned that Christianity affects your whole life. It's not just what happens inside the church building on a Sunday morning. There finally came a point, when I was without a job for the third time, that things gelled in my thinking.

In the midst of the crisis I realised that there was more to life than what I had experienced up to that time."

Heather says: "It was after I read a book by Cliff Richard that I realised there was such a thing as a personal faith in God. This was quite a revelation for me. I realised that I was completely separated from God, not due to my being a big-time sinner, but because of my wrong thoughts, gossip and petty selfishness. I came to a crisis-point at which I just poured out all these things to God and asked his forgiveness. That was the real turning point for me."

John continues: "We've always had a good marriage, but it's definitely become better since we've understood what it means to have a personal faith. I've certainly become more tolerant! Life hasn't been easier since becoming a Christian, but it's certainly been more fulfilling."

WASN'T JESUS JUST A GOOD MAN?

If Jesus was only a good man, why did he claim to be equal with God? The Christian writer, C.S. Lewis, once summed up the alternatives we have in responding to Jesus' claims:

"I am trying here to prevent anyone saying the really foolish thing that people often say about him: 'I'm ready to accept Jesus as a moral teacher, but I don't accept his claim to be God.' That is one thing we must not say. A man who was merely a man and said the sort of things that Jesus said would not be a great moral teacher. He would either be a lunatic – on a level with the man who says he is a poached egg – or else he would be the Devil of Hell. You must make your choice. Either this man was, and is, the Son of God; or else a madman or something worse. You can shut him up for a demon, or you can fall at his feet and call him Lord. But don't come up with any patronising nonsense about him being a great moral teacher. He hasn't left that alternative open to us."

You might think that anyone can claim to be God. There have been people who have declared themselves to be God, but in time have been shown up as rogues or madmen. The evidence of the way they lived did not support their claims. What makes Jesus unique is that the way he lived gives us good reason to believe that what he said was true. Jesus' character and work supports his words in a way we see in no other human life.

What's all this about sin? See page 48.

See the Identity pages in the Question and Answer section on www.rejesus.co.uk/the_story

your own followers use to force them out? They are the ones who will judge you. But if I use God's power to force out demons, it proves that God's kingdom has already come to you.

When a strong man arms himself and guards his home, everything he owns is safe. But if a stronger man comes and defeats him, he will carry off the weapons in which the strong man trusted. Then he will divide with others what he has taken. If you are not on my side, you are against me. If you don't gather in the crop with me, you scatter it.

Return of an Evil Spirit
When an evil spirit leaves a person, it travels through the desert, looking for a place to rest. But when it doesn't find a place, it says, "I'll go back to the home I left." When it gets there and finds the place clean and tidied up, it goes off and finds seven other evil spirits even worse than itself. They all come and make their home there, and that person ends up in worse shape than before.

Being Really Blessed
While Jesus was still talking, a woman in the crowd spoke up, "The woman who gave birth to you and fed you is blessed!"

Jesus replied, "That's true, but the people who are really blessed are the ones who hear and obey God's message!"

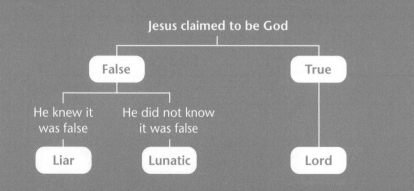

A Sign from God

As crowds were gathering around Jesus, he said:

You people of today are evil! You keep looking for a sign from God. But what happened to Jonah is the only sign you will be given. Just as Jonah was a sign to the people of Nineveh, the Son of Man will be a sign to the people of today. When the judgment comes, the Queen of the South will stand there with you and condemn you. She travelled a long way to hear Solomon's wisdom, and yet here is something far greater than Solomon. The people of Nineveh will also stand there with you and condemn you. They turned to God when Jonah preached, and yet here is something far greater than Jonah.

Light

No one lights a lamp and then hides it or puts it under a clay pot. A lamp is put on a lampstand, so that everyone who comes into the house can see the light. Your eyes are the lamp for your body. When your eyes are good, you have all the light you need. But when your eyes are bad, everything is dark. So be sure that your light isn't darkness. If you have light, and nothing is dark, then light will be everywhere, as when a lamp shines brightly on you.

Jesus Condemns the Pharisees and Teachers of the Law of Moses

When Jesus finished speaking, a Pharisee* invited him home for a meal. Jesus went and sat down to eat. The Pharisee was surprised that he didn't wash his hands before eating. So the Lord said to him:

You Pharisees clean the outside of cups and dishes, but on the inside you are greedy and evil. You fools! Didn't God make both the outside and the inside? If you would only give what you have to the poor, everything you do would please God.

You Pharisees are in for trouble! You give God a tenth of the spices from your gardens, such as mint and rue. But you cheat people, and you don't love God. You should be

"You are in for trouble"

fair and kind to others and still give a tenth to God.

You Pharisees are in for trouble! You love the front seats in the meeting places, and you like to be greeted with honour in the market. But you are in for trouble! You are like unmarked graves that people walk on without even knowing it.

A teacher of the Law of Moses spoke up, "Teacher, you said cruel things about us."

Jesus replied:

You teachers are also in for trouble! You load people down with heavy burdens, but

* PHARISEE

The Pharisees were an exclusive and influential Jewish religious party which prided itself on strict observance of Jewish law and the hundreds of interpretations added to it through the centuries. "Pharisee" literally means "a separated one". There were about 6000 Pharisees at the time of Jesus. Some responded positively to Jesus and his message, but as a whole they were among his fiercest opponents, eventually succeeding, through collaboration with others, in condemning him to death.

> "Always, always, always without relief there's this black hole inside and it never goes away."
> *Bob Geldof*

you won't lift a finger to help them carry the loads. Yes, you are really in for trouble. You build monuments to honour the prophets your own people murdered long ago. You must think that was the right thing for your people to do, or else you wouldn't have built monuments for the prophets they murdered.

Because of your evil deeds, the Wisdom of God said, "I will send prophets and apostles to you. But you'll murder some and mistreat others." You people living today will be punished for all the prophets who have been murdered since the beginning of the world. This includes every prophet from the time of Abel to the time of Zechariah, who was murdered between the altar and the temple. You people will certainly be punished for all of this.

You teachers of the Law of Moses are really in for trouble! You carry the keys to the door of knowledge about God. But you never go in, and you keep others from going in.

Jesus was about to leave, but the teachers and the Pharisees wanted to get even with him. They tried to make him say what he thought about other things, so that they could catch him saying something wrong.

Warnings

As thousands of people crowded around Jesus and were stepping on each other, he told his disciples:

Be sure to guard against the dishonest teaching of the Pharisees! It is their way of fooling people. Everything that is hidden will be found out, and every secret will be known. Whatever you say in the dark will be heard when it is day. Whatever you whisper in a closed room will be shouted from the housetops.

The One To Fear

My friends, don't be afraid of people. They can kill you, but after that, there is nothing else they can do. God is the one you must fear. Not only can he take your life, but he can throw you into hell. God is certainly the one you should fear!

Five sparrows are sold for just two small coins, but God doesn't forget one of them. Even the hairs on your head are counted. So don't be afraid! You are worth much more than many sparrows.

Telling Others about Christ

If you tell others that you belong to me, the Son of Man will tell God's angels that you are my followers. But if you reject me, you will be rejected in front of them. If you speak against the Son of Man, you can be forgiven, but if you speak against the Holy Spirit, you can't be forgiven.

When you are brought to trial in the Jewish meeting places or before rulers or officials, don't worry about how you will defend yourselves or what you will say. At that time the Holy Spirit will tell you what to say.

A Rich Fool

A man in a crowd said to Jesus, "Teacher, tell my brother to give me my share of what our father left us when he died."

Jesus answered, "Who gave me the right to settle arguments between you and your brother?"

Then he said to the crowd, "Don't be greedy! Owning a lot of things won't make your life safe."

So Jesus told them this story:

A rich man's farm produced a big crop, and he said to himself, "What can I do? I haven't got a place large enough to store everything."

Later, he said, "Now I know what I'll do. I'll tear down my barns and build bigger ones, where I can store all my grain and other goods. Then I'll say

to myself, 'You've stored up enough good things to last for years to come. Live it up! Eat, drink, and enjoy yourself."

But God said to him, "You fool! Tonight you will die. Then who will get what you have stored up?"

"This is what happens to people who store up everything for themselves, but are poor in the sight of God."

Worry
Jesus said to his disciples:

I tell you not to worry about your life! Don't worry about having something to eat or wear. Life is more than food or clothing. Look at the crows! They don't plant or harvest, and they don't have storehouses or barns. But God takes care of them. You are much more important than any birds. Can worry make you live longer? If you don't have power over small things, why worry about everything else?

"Your heart will always be where your treasure is"

Look how the wild flowers grow! They don't work hard to make their clothes. But I tell you that Solomon with all his wealth wasn't as well clothed as one of these flowers. God gives such beauty to everything that grows in the fields, even though it's here today and thrown into a fire tomorrow. Won't he do even more for you? You have such little faith!

Don't keep worrying about having something to eat or drink. Only people who don't know God are always worrying about such things. Your Father knows what you need. But put God's work first, and these things will be yours as well.

Treasures in Heaven
My little group of disciples, don't be afraid! Your Father wants to give you the kingdom. Sell what you have and give the money to the poor. Make yourselves moneybags that never wear out. Make sure your treasure is safe in heaven, where thieves can't steal it and moths can't destroy it. Your heart will always be where your treasure is.

Faithful and Unfaithful Servants
Be ready and keep your lamps burning just like those servants who wait up for their master to return from a wedding feast. As soon as he comes and knocks, they open the door for him. Servants are fortunate if their master finds them awake and ready when he comes! I promise you that he will get ready and make his servants sit down so that he can serve them. Those

* PARABLES

Jesus used stories, sometimes called 'parables', a great deal in his teaching. The word comes from a Greek word, meaning 'a comparison'. Jesus used stories about familiar everyday events as a way of illustrating particular truths. Parables usually have one main point. The details in the story are there to make it interesting to listen to.

servants are really fortunate if their master finds them ready, even though he comes late at night or early in the morning. You would surely not let a thief break into your home, if you knew when the thief was coming. So always be ready! You don't know when the Son of Man will come.

Peter asked Jesus, "Did you say this just for us or for everyone?"*

The Lord answered:

Who are faithful and wise servants? Who are the ones the master will put in charge of giving the other servants their food supplies at the proper time? Servants are fortunate if their master comes and finds them doing their job. A servant who is always faithful will surely be put in

"I came to make people choose sides"

charge of everything the master owns.

But suppose one of the servants thinks that the master won't return until late. Suppose that servant starts beating all the other servants and eats and drinks and gets drunk. If that happens, the master will come on a day and at a time when the servant least expects him. That servant will then be punished and thrown out with the servants who can't be trusted.

If servants are not ready or willing to do what their master wants them to do, they will be beaten hard. But servants who don't know what their master wants them to do won't be beaten so hard for doing wrong. If God has been generous with you, he will expect you to serve him well. But if he has been more than generous, he will expect you to serve him even better.

Not Peace, but Trouble

I came to set fire to the earth, and I wish it was already on fire! I am going to be put to a hard test. And I will have to suffer a lot of pain until it's over. Do you think that I came to bring peace to earth? No indeed! I came to make people choose sides. A family of five will be divided, with two of them against the other three. Fathers and sons will turn against one another, and mothers and daughters will do the same. Mothers-in-law and daughters-in-law will also turn against each other.

Knowing What To Do

Jesus said to all the people:

As soon as you see a cloud coming up in the west, you say, "It's going to rain," and it does. When the south wind blows, you say, "It's going to get hot," and it does. Are you trying to fool someone? You can predict the weather by looking at the earth and sky, but you don't really know what's going on right now. Why don't you understand the right thing to do? When someone accuses you of something, try to settle things before you are taken to court. If you don't, you will be dragged before the judge. Then the judge will hand you over to the jailer, and you will be locked up. You won't get out until you have paid the last penny you owe.

Life Story

ANDREA FARLEY

She had three major heart operations and a serious back operation all before the age of sixteen. When these experiences could have brought despair and depression, Andrea's trust in God and joy in the Christian life increased.

At the age of thirteen she was admitted to the local hospital and two months later transferred to Guy's Hospital in London. The doctors diagnosed her physical problem and loss of weight as a result of heart failure. Her disintegrating heart valve would need to be replaced.

She was so weak by this time she was only given a 50/50 chance of survival.

"For me, the incredible bit was that I recovered from the surgery so quickly. All my church was praying for me. About a week after the operation I was walking around, making jam tarts, going to hospital parties and everything. After that I began to realise how powerful God was."

Unfortunately her heart condition had caused her back to go into an S-shape which meant yet another operation, this time to fit two metal rods to her spine.

"For about five days I was in total agony. I didn't want to speak to anybody. I was told that I was expected to be in hospital for about a month and then to go home on crutches. In fact I came out exactly a week after the operation and I walked without crutches. The doctors and nurses were amazed."

"People say to me 'Why didn't God heal you?' I'm not altogether sure, but I believe that God knows best. He's taught me so much through being in pain that I find when I talk to other people, I can really say and mean it 'I know how you feel'. Although I wasn't healed, it doesn't matter, because I had an incredible recovery and I knew God was with me. It's made me realise that nothing is too small or too big to talk to God about. Whatever the situation, no matter how bad it is, God can use it."

LOST & FOUND

About this same time Jesus was told that Pilate had given orders for some people from Galilee to be killed while they were offering sacrifices.

Jesus replied:

Do you think that these people were worse sinners than everyone else in Galilee just because of what happened to them? Not at all! But you can be sure that if you don't turn back to God, every one of you will also be killed. What about those people who died when the tower in Siloam fell on them? Do you think they were worse than everyone else in Jerusalem? Not at all! But you can be sure that if you don't turn back to God, every one of you will also die.

A Story about a Fig Tree
Jesus then told them this story:

A man had a fig tree growing in his vineyard. One day he went out to pick some figs, but he didn't find any. So he said to the gardener, "For three years I have come looking for figs on this tree, and I haven't found any yet. Chop it down! Why should it take up space?"

The gardener answered, "Master, leave it for another year. I'll dig around it and put some manure on it to make it grow. Maybe it will have figs on it next year. If it doesn't, you can have it cut down."

Healing a Woman on the Sabbath*
One Sabbath, Jesus was teaching in a Jewish meeting place, and a woman was there who had been crippled by an evil spirit for years. She was completely bent over and couldn't straighten up. When

Jesus saw the woman, he called her over and said, "You are now well." He placed his hands on her, and at once she stood up straight and praised God.

The man in charge of the meeting place was angry because Jesus had healed someone on the Sabbath. So he said to the people, "Each week has six days when we can work. Come and be healed on one of those days, but not on the Sabbath." The Lord replied,

"Are you trying to fool someone? Won't any one of you untie your bullock or donkey and lead it out to drink on a Sabbath? This woman belongs to the family of Abraham, but Satan has kept her bound for years. Isn't it right to set her free on the Sabbath?" Jesus' words made his enemies ashamed. But everyone else in the crowd was happy about the wonderful things he was doing.

A Mustard Seed and Yeast
Jesus said, "What is God's kingdom like? What can I compare it with? It is like what happens when someone plants a mustard seed in a garden. The seed grows as big as a tree, and birds nest in its branches."

Then Jesus said, "What can I compare God's kingdom with? It is like what happens when a woman mixes yeast into three batches of flour. Finally, all the dough rises."

The Narrow Door
As Jesus was on his way to Jerusalem, he taught the people in the towns and villages. Someone asked him, "Lord, are only a few people going to be saved?"

Jesus answered:

Do all you can to go in by the narrow door! A lot of people will try to get in, but won't be able to. Once the owner of the house gets up

> ## "Are only a few people going to be saved?"

and locks the door, you will be left standing outside. You will knock on the door and say, "Sir, open the door for us!" But the owner will answer, "I don't know a thing about you!"

Then you will start saying, "We dined with you, and you taught in our streets."

But he will say, "I really don't know who you are! Get away from me, you evil people!"

Then when you have been thrown outside, you will weep and grit your teeth because you will see Abraham and Isaac and all the prophets in God's kingdom. People will come from all directions and sit down to feast in God's kingdom. There the ones who are now least important will be the most important, and those who are now most important will be least important.

Jesus and Herod
At that time some Pharisees came to Jesus and said, "You had better get away from here! Herod wants to kill you." Jesus said to them:

Go and tell that fox, "I am going to force out demons and heal people today and tomorrow, and three days later I'll be finished." But I am going on my way today and tomorrow and the next day. After all, Jerusalem is the place where prophets are killed.

Jesus Loves Jerusalem
Jerusalem, Jerusalem! Your people have killed the prophets and have stoned the messengers who were sent to you. I have often wanted to gather your people, as a hen gathers her chickens under her wings. But you wouldn't let me. Now your temple will be deserted. You won't see me again until the time when you say,

"Blessed is the one who comes in the name of the Lord."

* MIRACLES
Through parables Jesus taught people about the Kingdom of God. Jesus' miracles show God's rule in action. They express his compassion for those in need. Jesus' miracles were also the weapon he used to combat the activity of Satan, freeing people from the power of evil to live under the rule of God. Like sign posts, they point to who he was, revealing his glory and power as the Son of God.

Jeruselem today

HAT'S ALL THIS ABOUT SIN?

Sin is an attitude of rebellion or indifference towards God. It results in doing wrong or failing to do right. At root it means falling short of God's standard. The consequence is that we cut ourselves off from God and heaven.

Many would argue, "but surely God will excuse me if I have tried my best? And anyway, I'm not as bad as others. I'm OK."

Jesus would have not agreed.

While Jesus demonstrated love to people who had failed, he was nevertheless uncompromising about sin. He said that sin includes the way we think, not just what we do. "Out of your heart come evil thoughts, vulgar deeds, stealing murder, unfaithfulness in marriage, greed, meanness, deceit, indecency, envy, insults, pride and foolishness. All these come from your heart, and they are what make you unfit to worship God." (Mark 7 v 20-23) No one is innocent.

Our attitude to God is crucial. Whether we have achieved it or not, our aim is to have life the way we want it. We've gone our way rather than God's way. For many of us God is an irrelevance. We live as if he didn't exist. For others, he plays a part, but he does not have the place he deserves.

This attitude of rebellion or indifference is serious. It cannot be brushed aside. The rift between us and God cannot be solved by any amount of good behaviour.

Is there a way for sinful people to experience God's love and forgiveness?

How is Jesus' death a solution for sin? See page 54.

See www.rejesus.co.uk/startagain

Jesus Heals a Sick Man

One Sabbath, Jesus was having dinner in the home of an important Pharisee, and everyone was carefully watching Jesus. All of a sudden a man with swollen legs stood up in front of him. Jesus turned and asked the Pharisees and the teachers of the Law of Moses, "Is it right to heal on the Sabbath?" But they didn't say a word.

"If you put yourself above others, you will be put down"

Jesus took hold of the man. Then he healed him and sent him away. Afterwards, Jesus asked the people, "If your son or your bullock falls into a well, wouldn't you pull him out straight away, even on the Sabbath?" There was nothing they could say.

How To Be a Guest

Jesus saw how the guests had tried to take the best seats. So he told them:

When you are invited to a wedding feast, don't sit in the best place. Someone more important may have been invited. Then the one who invited you will come and say, "Give your place to this other guest!" You will be embarrassed and will have to sit in the worst place.

When you are invited to be a guest, go and sit in the worst place. Then the one who invited you may come and say, "My friend, take a better seat!" You will then be honoured in front of all the other guests. If you put yourself above others, you will be put down. But if you humble yourself, you will be honoured.

Then Jesus said to the man who had invited him:

When you give a dinner or a banquet, don't invite your friends and family and relatives and rich neighbours. If you do, they will invite you in return, and you will be paid back. When you give a feast, invite the poor, the crippled, the lame, and the blind. They can't pay you back. But God will bless you and reward you when his people rise from death.

The Great Banquet

After Jesus had finished speaking, one of the guests said, "The greatest blessing of all is to be at the banquet in God's kingdom!"

Jesus told him:

A man once gave a great banquet and invited a lot of guests. When the banquet was ready, he sent a servant to tell the guests, "Everything is ready! Please come."

One guest after another started making excuses. The first one said, "I bought some land, and I've got to look it over. Please excuse me."

Another guest said, "I bought five teams of bullocks, and I need to try them out. Please excuse me."

Still another guest said, "I've just got married, and I can't be there."

The servant told his master what happened, and the master became so angry that he said, "Go as fast as you can to every street and alley in town! Bring in everyone who is poor or crippled or blind or lame."

When the servant returned, he said, "Master, I've done what you told me, and there is still plenty room for more people."

His master then told him, "Go out along the back roads and tracks and make people come in, so that my house will be full. Not one of the guests I first invited will get even a bite of my food!"

Being a Disciple

Large crowds were walking along with Jesus, when he turned and said:

You can't be my disciple, unless you love me more than you love your father and mother, your wife and children, and your brothers and sisters. You can't come with me unless you love me more than you love your own life.

"This man is friendly with sinners"

You can't be my disciple unless you carry your own cross and come with me.

Suppose one of you wants to build a tower. What is the first thing you will do? Won't you sit down and work out how much it will cost and if you have enough money to pay for it? Otherwise, you will start building the tower, but not be able to finish. Then everyone who sees what is happening will laugh at you. They will say, "You started building, but couldn't finish the job."

What will a king do if he has only 10,000 soldiers to defend himself against a king who is about to attack him with 20,000 soldiers? Before he goes out to battle, won't he first sit down and decide if he can win? If he thinks he won't be able to defend himself, he will send messengers and ask for peace while the other king is still a long way off. So then, you can't be my disciple unless you give away everything you own.

"It's pride that says, "I'll make myself good enough first.""
Delia Smith

> "The supreme happiness of life is the conviction that we are loved."
> *Victor Hugo*

Salt and Light

Salt is good, but if it no longer tastes like salt, how can it be made to taste salty again? It is no longer good for the soil or even for the manure pile. People simply throw it out. If you have ears, pay attention!

One Sheep

Tax collectors and sinners were all crowding around to listen to Jesus. So the Pharisees and the teachers of the Law of Moses started grumbling, "This man is friendly with sinners. He even eats with them."

Then Jesus told them this story:

If any of you has 100 sheep, and one of them gets lost, what will you do? Won't you leave the 99 in the field and go and look for the lost sheep until you find it? And when you find it, you will be so glad that you will put it on your shoulder and carry it home. Then you will call in your friends and neighbours and say, "Let's celebrate! I've found my lost sheep."

Jesus said, "In the same way there is more happiness in heaven because of one sinner who turns to God than over 99 good people who don't need to."

One Coin

Jesus told the people another story:

What will a woman do if she has ten silver coins and loses one of them? Won't she light a lamp, sweep the floor, and look carefully until she finds it? Then she will call in her friends and neighbours and say, "Let's celebrate! I've found the coin I lost."

Jesus said, "In the same way God's angels are happy when even one person turns to him."

Two Sons

Jesus also told them another story:

Once a man had two sons. The younger son said to his father, "Give me my share of the property." So the father divided his property between his two sons.

Not long after that, the younger son packed up everything he owned and left for a foreign country, where he wasted all his money in wild living. He had spent everything, when a bad famine spread through that whole land. Soon he had nothing to eat.

He went to work for a man in that country, and the man sent him out to take care of his pigs. He would have been glad to eat what the pigs were eating, but no one gave him a thing.

Finally, he came to his senses and said, "My father's workers have plenty to eat, and here I am, starving to death! I will go to my father and say to him, 'Father, I've sinned against God in heaven and against you. I'm no longer good enough to be called your son. Treat me like one of your workers.'"

The younger son got up and started back to his father. But when he was still a long way off, his father saw him and felt sorry for him. He ran to his son and hugged and kissed him.

The son said, "Father, I've sinned against God in heaven and against you. I'm no longer good enough to be called your son."

But his father said to the servants, "Hurry and bring the best clothes and put them on him. Give him a ring for his finger and sandals for his feet. Get the best calf and prepare it, so we can eat and celebrate. This son of mine was dead, but has now come back to life. He was lost and has now been found." And they began to celebrate.

The older son had been out in the field. But when he came near the house, he heard the music and dancing. So he called one of the servants over and asked, "What's going on here?"

The servant answered, "Your brother has come home safe and sound, and your father ordered us to kill the best calf." The older brother got so angry that he wouldn't even go into the house.

His father came out and

begged him to go in. But he said to his father, "For years I've worked for you like a slave and have always obeyed you. But you have never even given me a little goat, so that I could give a dinner for my friends. This other son of yours wasted your money on prostitutes. And now that he has come home, you ordered the best calf to be killed for a feast."

His father replied, "My son, you're always with me, and everything I have is yours. But we should be glad and celebrate! Your brother was dead, but he's now alive. He was lost and has now been found."

MENINA JONES

Life Story

Boys in Israel today

"To me God was someone who I mostly feared. I had to be good and if not I would be punished."

Menina Jones is a retired school teacher. She was born in Bari, Italy but now lives in the UK.

"I was brought up a Catholic and went regularly to church. When at the age of 22 I lost my first child, I was absolutely shattered. My immediate reaction was that I had been punished for something. What had I done to deserve such unbearable punishment? I was angry, I thought God was unjust if he could do that to me. I felt abandoned and so full of rebellion! If he did not love me, I could well do without him. I think I still believed in him but he was just somewhere 'out there'."

"I had what we call a satisfying life; a lovely family, a comfortable home, a job I enjoyed. But so often I felt dissatisfied. My life felt empty and meaningless."

"My son Glynn became a Christian in his late teens and I am ashamed to say that I never helped or encouraged him. Yet he became my link with Jesus. It was through Glynn, and later his wife Monica, that I eventually found God. They never tried to push anything on to me, but I listened to them and sometimes asked questions. I wanted to find the peace and serenity that they had, because I knew I didn't have it."

"In time I realised God wasn't the being I had feared all my life, but he loved me and forgave me. As I became more convinced of his love I found I could talk to him, rather than just say the fixed prayers I had always said before. If I have moments when I feel down and low, I just talk to God. I know he listens to me, just as if he was sitting beside me. I hope I'm a better person now. I've got more patience and I'm more tolerant of others and I hope I can show my love to other people. God has really changed my life and given me peace."

PLANNING FOR THE FUTURE

Jesus said to his disciples: A rich man once had a manager to take care of his business. But he was told that his manager was wasting money. So the rich man called him in and said, "What is this I hear about you? Tell me what you have done! You are no longer going to work for me."

The manager said to himself, "What shall I do now that my master is going to fire me? I can't dig ditches, and I'm ashamed to beg. I know what I'll do, so that people will welcome me into their homes after I've lost my job."

Then one by one he called in the people who were in debt to his master. He asked the first one, "How much do you owe my master?"

"100 barrels of olive oil," the man answered.

So the manager said, "Take your bill and sit down and quickly write '50'."

"You can't serve God and money"

The manager asked someone else who was in debt to his master, "How much do you owe?"

"1000 bags of wheat," the man replied.

The manager said, "Take your bill and write '800'."

The master praised his dishonest manager for looking after himself so well. That's how it is! The people of this world look after themselves better than the people who belong to the light.

My disciples, I tell you to use wicked wealth to make friends for yourselves. Then when it is gone, you will be welcomed into an eternal home. Anyone who can be trusted in little matters can also be trusted in important matters. But anyone who is dishonest in little matters will be dishonest in important matters. If you can't be trusted

with this wicked wealth, who will trust you with true wealth? And if you can't be trusted with what belongs to someone else, who will give you something that will be your own? You can't be the slave of two masters. You will like one more than the other or be more loyal to one than to the other. You can't serve God and money.

Some Sayings of Jesus

The Pharisees really loved money. So when they heard what Jesus said, they made fun of him. But Jesus told them:

You are always making yourselves look good, but God sees what is in your heart. The things that most people think are important are worthless as far as God is concerned.

Until the time of John the Baptist, people had to obey the Law of Moses and the Books of the Prophets. But since God's kingdom has been preached, everyone is trying hard to get in. Heaven and earth will disappear before the smallest letter of the Law does.

It is a terrible sin for a man to divorce his wife and marry another woman. It is also a terrible sin for a man to marry a divorced woman.

Lazarus and the Rich Man

There was once a rich man who wore expensive clothes and every day ate the best food. But a poor beggar named Lazarus was brought to the gate of the rich man's house. He was happy just to eat the scraps that fell from the rich man's table. His body was covered with sores, and dogs kept coming up to lick them. The poor man died, and angels took him to the place of honour next to Abraham.

The rich man also died and was buried. He went to hell and was suffering terribly. When he looked up and saw Abraham far off and Lazarus at his side, he said to Abraham, "Have pity on me! Send Lazarus to dip his finger in water and touch my tongue. I'm suffering terribly in this fire."

Abraham answered, "My friend, remember that while you lived, you had everything good, and Lazarus had everything bad. Now he is happy, and you are in pain. And besides, there is a deep valley between us, and no one from either side can cross over."

But the rich man said, "Abraham, then please send Lazarus to my father's home. Let him warn my five brothers, so they won't come to this horrible place."

Abraham answered, "Your brothers can read what Moses and the prophets wrote. They should pay attention to that."

Then the rich man said, "No, that's not enough! If only someone from the dead would go to them, they would listen and turn to God."

So Abraham said, "If they won't pay attention to Moses and the prophets, they won't listen even to someone who comes back from the dead."

Faith and Service

Jesus said to his disciples:

There will always be something that causes people to sin. But anyone who causes them to sin is in for trouble. A person who causes even one of my little followers to sin would be better off thrown into the ocean with a heavy stone tied around their neck. So be careful what you do.

Correct any followers of mine who sin, and forgive the ones who say they are sorry. Even if one of them mistreats you seven times in one day and says, "I'm sorry," you should still forgive that person.

The apostles said to the Lord, "Make our faith stronger!"

Jesus replied:

If you had faith no bigger than a tiny mustard seed, you could tell this mulberry tree to pull itself up, roots and all, and to plant itself in the

> "I'm not afraid to die. I just don't want to be there when it happens."
> *Woody Allen*

HOW IS JESUS' DEATH THE SOLUTION FOR SIN?

If sin is the root of the problem that afflicts us all, how can the death of one man be the solution?

Sin distances us from God in this life. Death will cut us off from him forever. That is the natural consequence of our independence and rebellion. The only person who never rebelled against God, never put his will before God's, was Jesus. His relationship with God the Father need never have been broken. Death for him, would have been the gateway to an even closer contact with his Father in heaven.

Instead, at his death, Jesus willingly experienced the hell of total separation from God the Father that should have been ours. He took upon himself the consequence of our rebellion. Only he could have done that. As people who have chosen not to follow God's ways, there is nothing to our credit that we can offer to God. We are bankrupt. In contrast, Jesus had everything to offer – and he gave it all on our behalf rather than keeping it for himself.

God accepted Jesus' life and death on behalf of all people. That opened up the way for us to enter into a restored relationship with God. What is required from us is the readiness to accept what Jesus has done for us.

God's forgiveness is there for the taking for those who recognise that they need it. He is ready to receive those who are willing to acknowledge his rule in their lives.

This doesn't mean that Christians are completely free from the problem of sin, but once we accept the rule of God in our lives, we are under new management. God gives us the power to begin to live as free, forgiven people.

Through the death of Jesus, God has made it possible for us to come back where he has always meant us to be – with himself.

Is Jesus the only way to God? See page 60.

See the Life pages in the Question and Answer section on www. rejesus.co.uk/the_story

ocean. And it would!

If your servant comes in from ploughing or from taking care of the sheep, would you say, "Welcome! Come on in and have something to eat"? No, you wouldn't say that. You would say, "Make me something to eat. Get ready to serve me, so I can have my meal. Then later on you can eat and drink." Servants don't deserve special thanks for doing what they are supposed to do. And that's how it should be with you. When you have done all you should, then say, "We are merely servants, and we've simply done our duty."

Ten Men with Leprosy
On his way to Jerusalem, Jesus went along the border between Samaria and Galilee. As he was going into a village, ten men with leprosy came towards him. They stood at a distance and shouted, "Jesus, Master, have pity on us!"

Jesus looked at them and said, "Go and show yourselves to the priests."

On their way they were healed. When one of them discovered that he was healed, he came back, shouting praises to God. He bowed down at the feet of Jesus and thanked him. The man was from the country of Samaria.

Jesus asked, "Weren't ten men healed? Where are the other nine? Why was this foreigner the only one who came back to thank God?" Then Jesus told the man,

"You may get up and go. Your faith has made you well."

God's Kingdom

Some Pharisees asked Jesus when God's kingdom would come. He answered, "God's kingdom isn't something you can see. There is no use saying, 'Look! Here it is' or 'Look! There it is.' God's kingdom is here with you."

Jesus said to his disciples:

The time will come when you will long to see one of the days of the Son of Man, but you won't. When people say to you, "Look there," or "Look here," don't go looking for him. The day of the Son of Man will be like lightning flashing across the sky. But first he must suffer terribly and be rejected by the people of today. When the Son of Man comes, things will be just as they were when Noah lived. People were eating, drinking, and getting married right up to the day when Noah went into the big boat. Then the flood came and drowned everyone on earth.

When Lot lived, people were also eating and drinking. They were buying, selling, planting, and building. But on the very day Lot left Sodom, fiery flames poured down from the sky and killed everyone. The same will happen on the day when the Son of Man appears.

At that time no one on a rooftop should go down into the house to get anything. No one in a field should go back to the house for anything. Remember what happened to Lot's wife.

People who try to save their lives will lose them, and those who lose their lives will save them. On that night two people will be sleeping in the same bed, but only one will be taken. The other will be left. Two women will be together grinding wheat, but only one will be taken. The other will be left.

Then Jesus' disciples spoke up, "But where will this happen, Lord?"

Jesus said, "Where there is a corpse, there will always be vultures."

A Widow and a Judge

Jesus told his disciples a story about how they should keep on praying and never give up:

In a town there was once a judge who didn't fear God or care about people. In that same town there was a widow who kept going to the judge and saying, "Make sure that I get fair treatment in court."

For a while the judge refused to do anything. Finally, he said to himself, "Even though I don't fear God or care about people, I will help this widow because she keeps on bothering me. If I don't help her, she'll wear me out."

The Lord said:

Think about what that crooked judge said. Won't God protect his chosen ones who pray to him day and night? Won't he be concerned for them? He will surely hurry and help them. But when the Son of Man comes, will he find on this earth anyone with faith?

A Pharisee and a Tax Collector

Jesus told a story to some people who thought they were better than others and who looked down on everyone else:

Two men went into the temple to pray. One was a Pharisee and the other a tax collector. The Pharisee stood by himself and prayed, "God, I thank you that I am not greedy, dishonest, and unfaithful in marriage like other people. And I'm really glad that I'm not like that tax collector over there. I go without eating for two days a week, and I give you one tenth of all I earn."

The tax collector stood off at a distance and didn't think he was good enough even to

"I expect to win my battle against cancer, but no matter how it goes, I'm at peace with God. I can't lose."
Steve McQueen

> "Money won't buy happiness but it will pay the salaries of a large research staff to study the problem."
> *Bill Vaughan*

look up towards heaven. He was so sorry for what he had done that he pounded his chest and prayed, "God, have pity on me! I'm such a sinner."

Then Jesus said, "When the two men went home, it was the tax collector and not the Pharisee who was pleasing to God. If you put yourself above others, you will be put down. But if you humble yourself, you will be honoured."

Jesus Blesses Little Children

Some people brought their little children for Jesus to bless. But when his disciples saw them doing this, they told the people to stop bothering him. So Jesus called the children over to him and said, "Let the children come to me! Don't try to stop them. People who are like these children belong to God's kingdom. You will never get into God's kingdom unless you enter it like a child!"

A Rich and Important Man

An important man asked Jesus, "Good Teacher, what must I do to have eternal life?"

Jesus said, "Why do you call me good? Only God is good. You know the commandments: 'Be faithful in marriage. Do not murder. Do not steal. Do not tell lies about others. Respect your father and mother.'"

He told Jesus, "I've obeyed all these commandments since I was a young man."

When Jesus heard this, he said, "There is one thing you still need to do. Go and sell everything you own! Give the money to the poor, and you will have riches in heaven. Then come and be my follower." When the man heard this, he was sad, because he was very rich.

Jesus saw how sad the man was. So he said, "It's terribly hard for rich people to get into God's kingdom! In fact, it's easier for a camel to go through the eye of a needle than for a rich person to get into God's kingdom."

"It's terribly hard for rich people to get into God's kingdom!"

When the crowd heard this, they asked, "How can anyone ever be saved?"

Jesus replied, "There are some things that people can't do, but God can do anything."

Peter said, "Remember, we left everything to be your followers!"

Jesus answered, "You can be sure that anyone who gives up home or wife or brothers or family or children because of God's kingdom will be given much more in this life. And in the future world they will have eternal life."

"I was quite happy without God, driven by achieving my own goals, and being in control of my own life."

By his mid-30s Steven Skakel was already in a top management job. He had a beautiful wife and two lovely children. He could honestly say he'd achieved many of his life's goals.

"But then I started to ask myself questions like; 'Isn't there more to life than this?' 'What happens when I die?' and 'Is there really a God?' A friend invited me to a men's breakfast event where I heard a businessman speak about having a personal relationship with God. I was intrigued. It set me thinking about what I really considered important."

"So,... I took the plunge and joined a discussion group looking at Jesus. The things he said and did made me realise that my priorities were upside down. All my decisions were based on what would make life easier or happier for me and my family. I finally acknowledged that I was going about life my own way, that I needed God's forgiveness and that I truly wanted him at the centre of my life. Instead of pleasing myself, I wanted to please God. I was still caring for my family and getting on with my job but my focus was now on God."

"Jesus summarised the 10 commandments as: "Love the Lord your God with all your heart, soul, mind and strength and secondly love your neighbour as yourself" (Matthew 22:34-40) and this became my No 1 goal. There are a lot of people who will be able to tell you how many times I get it wrong – and that's only the times they can see me! But I am still learning and, as I allow him to, God is changing me bit by bit to live more by his priorities in my work and at home."

HEADING FOR TROUBLE

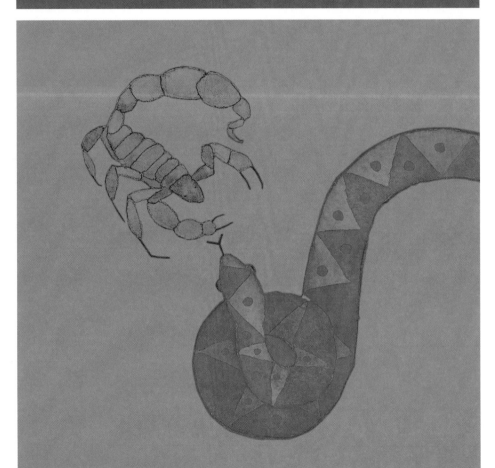

Jesus took the twelve apostles aside and said: We are now on our way to Jerusalem. Everything that the prophets wrote about the Son of Man will happen there.

He will be handed over to foreigners, who will make fun of him, mistreat him, and spit on him. They will beat him and kill him, but three days later he will rise to life. The apostles didn't understand what Jesus was talking about. They couldn't understand, because the meaning of what he said was hidden from them.

Jesus Heals a Blind Beggar
When Jesus was coming close to Jericho, a blind man sat begging beside the road. The man heard the crowd walking by and asked what was happening. Some people told him that Jesus from Nazareth was passing by. So the blind man shouted, "Jesus, Son of David, have pity on me!" The people who were going along with Jesus told the man to be quiet. But he shouted even louder, "Son of David, have pity on me!"

"What do you want me to do for you?"

Jesus stopped and told some people to bring the blind man over to him. When the blind man was getting near, Jesus asked, "What do you want me to do for you?"

"Lord, I want to see!" he answered.

Jesus replied, "Look and you will see! Your eyes are healed because of your faith." Straight away the man could see, and he went with Jesus and started thanking God. When the crowds saw what happened, they praised God.

Zacchaeus

Jesus was going through Jericho, where a man named Zacchaeus lived. He was in charge of collecting taxes* and was very rich. Jesus was heading his way, and Zacchaeus wanted to see what he was like. But Zacchaeus was a short man and couldn't see over the crowd. So he ran ahead and climbed up into a sycamore tree.

When Jesus got there, he looked up and said, "Zacchaeus, hurry down! I want to stay with you today." Zacchaeus hurried down and gladly welcomed Jesus.

Everyone who saw this started grumbling, "This man Zacchaeus is a sinner! And Jesus is going home to eat with him."

Later that day Zacchaeus stood up and said to the Lord, "I'll give half of my property to the poor. And I'll now pay back four times as much to everyone I've ever cheated."

Jesus said to Zacchaeus, "Today you and your family have been saved, because you are a true son of Abraham. The Son of Man came to look for and to save people who are lost."

A Story about Ten Servants

The crowd was still listening to Jesus as he was getting close to Jerusalem. Many of them thought that God's kingdom would soon appear, and Jesus told them this story:

A prince once went to a foreign country to be crowned king and then to return. But before leaving, he called in ten servants and gave each of them some money. He told them, "Use this to earn more money until I get back."

But the people of his country hated him, and they sent messengers to the foreign country to say, "We don't want this man to be our king."

After the prince had been made king, he returned and called in his servants. He asked them how much they had earned with the money they had been given.

The first servant came and said, "Sir, with the money you gave me I've earned ten times as much."

"That's fine, my good servant!" the king said. "Since you have shown that you can be trusted with a small amount, you will be given ten cities to rule."

The second one came and said, "Sir, with the money you gave me, I've earned five times as much."

The king said, "You will be given five cities."

Another servant came and said, "Sir, here is your money. I kept it safe in a handkerchief. You are a hard man, and I was afraid of you. You take what isn't yours, and you harvest crops you didn't plant."

"The Son of Man came to look for and to save people who are lost"

"You worthless servant!" the king told him. "You have condemned yourself by what you have just said. You knew that I'm a hard man, taking what isn't mine and harvesting what I haven't planted. Why didn't you put my money in the bank? On my return, I could have had the money together with interest."

Then he said to some other servants standing there, "Take the money away from him

* COLLECTING TAXES

The tax collectors were Jews, hated by their countrymen because they worked for the Romans. They usually collected more than the Romans wanted in taxes so that they had plenty left over for themselves. Zacchaeus was a chief tax collector and probably very wealthy. Many people would have disapproved of Jesus making friends with a man like this.

IS JESUS THE ONLY WAY TO GOD?

If all religions lead to God, then they should agree on fundamental issues. In fact they do not. Some say God is a person; others that there are many gods; others that God is just an impersonal force. Some say we live once, and then are judged; others say that we come back for life after life. Some claim this world is real; others claim that "reality" is just an illusion. If all religions have an equal claim to be believed we're no wiser than when we first started, because they contradict each other.

If all religions lead to God, you would expect he would have made the signposts to find him clearer. What kind of God would allow this sort of confusion to continue? Hindus believe one thing, the Muslims another, Christians something else. They all disagree. Surely God would make it clear? He did. Jesus said that he came from God to show us what God is like.

Jesus claims to be unique. He said "I am the way and the truth and the life, no-one comes to the Father except through me" (John 14:6). Is it intolerant to say that one religion is true? Truth by its very nature is exclusive: if one thing is true, then the opposite is not. If this statement is true it is not intolerant of Christians to say that Jesus is the only way to God.

Did Jesus rise from the dead? See page 75.

Take a look at some of evidence again… See the Question and Answer section on www.rejesus.co.uk/the_story

and give it to the servant who earned ten times as much."

But they said, "Sir, he already has ten times as much!"

The king replied, "Those who have something will be given more. But everything will be taken away from those who don't have anything. Now bring me the enemies who didn't want me to be their king. Kill them while I watch!"

Jesus Enters Jerusalem

When Jesus had finished saying all this, he went on towards Jerusalem. As he was getting near Bethphage and Bethany on the Mount of Olives, he sent two of his disciples on ahead. He told them, "Go into the next village, where you will find a young donkey that has never been ridden. Untie the donkey and bring it here. If anyone asks why you are doing that, just say, 'The Lord needs it.'"

They went off and found everything just as Jesus had said. While they were untying the donkey, its owners asked, "Why are you doing that?"

They answered, "The Lord needs it."

Then they led the donkey to Jesus. They put some of their clothes on its back and helped Jesus get on. And as he rode along, the people spread clothes on the road in front of him. When Jesus was starting down the Mount of Olives, his large crowd of disciples were happy and praised God because of all the miracles they had seen.

They shouted,
"Blessed is the king who comes in the name of the Lord!

Peace in heaven and glory to God."

Some Pharisees in the crowd said to Jesus, "Teacher, make your disciples stop shouting!"

But Jesus answered, "If they keep quiet, these stones will start shouting."

When Jesus came closer and could see Jerusalem, he cried and said:

It is too bad that today your people don't know what will bring them peace! Now it is hidden from them. Jerusalem, the time will come when your enemies will build walls around you to attack you. Armies will surround you and close in on you from every side. They will level you to the ground and kill your people. Not one stone in your buildings will be left on top of another. This will happen because you didn't see that God had come to save you.

Jesus in the Temple

When Jesus entered the temple, he started chasing out the people who were selling things. He told them, "The Scriptures say, 'My house should be a place of worship.' But you have made it a place where robbers hide!"

Each day, Jesus kept on teaching in the temple. So the chief priests*, the teachers of the Law of Moses, and some other important people tried to have him killed. But they couldn't find a way to do it, because everyone else was eager to listen to him.

A Question about Jesus' Authority

One day, Jesus was teaching in the temple and telling the good news. So the chief priests, the teachers, and the nation's leaders asked him, "What right have you got to do these things? Who gave you this authority?"

"Who gave you this authority?"

Jesus replied, "I want to ask you a question. Who gave John the right to baptise? Was it God in heaven or merely some human being?"

They talked this over and said to each other, "We can't say that God gave John this right. Jesus will ask us why we didn't believe John. And we can't say that it was merely some human who gave John the right to baptise. The crowd will stone us to death, because they think John was a prophet."

So they told Jesus, "We don't know who gave John the right to baptise."

Jesus replied, "Then I won't tell you who gave me the right to do what I do."

Tenants of a Vineyard

Jesus told the people this story:

A man once planted a vineyard and rented it out. Then he left the country for a long time. When it was time to harvest the crop, he sent a servant to ask the tenants for his share of the grapes. But they beat up the servant and sent him away without anything. So the owner sent another servant. The tenants also beat him up. They insulted him terribly and sent him away without a thing. The owner sent a third servant. He was also beaten terribly and thrown out of the vineyard.

The owner then said to himself, "What am I going to do? I know what. I'll send my son, the one I love so much. They will surely respect him!"

When the tenants saw the owner's son, they said to one another, "Some day he will own the vineyard. Let's kill him! Then we can have it all for ourselves." So they threw him out of the vineyard and killed him.

Jesus asked, "What do you think the owner of the vineyard will do? I'll tell you what. He will come and kill those tenants and let someone else have his vineyard."

When the people heard this, they said, "This must never happen!"

But Jesus looked straight at them and said, "Then what do the Scriptures mean when they say, 'The stone that the builders tossed aside is now the most important stone of all'? Anyone who stumbles over this stone will get hurt, and anyone it falls on will be smashed to pieces."

The chief priests and the teachers of the Law of Moses knew that Jesus was talking about them when he was telling this story. They wanted to arrest him straight away, but they were afraid of the people.

Paying Taxes

Jesus' enemies kept watching him closely, because they wanted to hand him over to the Roman governor. So they sent some men who pretended to be good. But they were really spies trying to catch Jesus saying something wrong. The spies said to him, "Teacher, we know that you teach the truth about what God wants people to do. And you treat everyone with the same respect, no matter who they are. Tell us, should we pay taxes to the Emperor or not?"

Jesus knew that they were trying to trick him. So he told them, "Show me a coin." Then he asked, "Whose picture and name are on it?"

* CHIEF PRIESTS

The chief priests controlled the ruling council of the Jews. They mainly belonged to the religious group called the Sadducees, one of the key religious and political groups of Jesus' time. This group came largely from the wealthy landowners or aristocracy.

The walls of Jerusalem

Life Story

AHMED MOHAMMED

Ahmed Mohammed was born in Iran and brought up a God-fearing Muslim.

"The only God I knew then was the one in the Quran (Koran); a holy, great and powerful being, against whom I felt small and sinful. I wanted to be a friend of God, but this seemed impossible because of his greatness and my sin. At secondary school I put thoughts of God behind me and got on with life."

"In my first job I met someone who was always talking about Christianity. I told this colleague that Islam was superior to Christianity, that the Quran is the last message from God and that Mohammed was the last prophet. We argued a lot. Eventually the office manager said that this was not the place for religious discussion; 'Go to the church, or the mosque, and continue the discussion there.' We tossed a coin and the church won."

"I was so convinced I was right that I told the people at church that it should be turned into a mosque. I behaved very arrogantly toward the pastor, but he was very welcoming. I asked him what he thought about the Quran. He replied, 'This is

a church. I am the pastor. I can only answer questions about the Bible and Jesus.' So I asked him to tell me about Jesus, because I knew that he was one of the prophets."

"He told me that God loved me. I could not see why God should want to love me. He went on to explain that Jesus came to die on the cross for me. I began to go to the church a few times every week. Gradually I stopped asking questions about Mohammed and concentrated on finding out more about Jesus. I started reading the New Testament."

"After about six months, the pastor said 'You know enough now to decide whether you will follow Jesus. Find a quiet place at home to pray to him.' I did this saying, 'Jesus, I know you are alive. Please come into my heart, change my life and stay with me.'"

"Two years later I married the colleague who had first talked to me about Jesus."

(Ahmed's name has been changed to protect his family)

"Give God what belongs to God"

"The Emperor's," they answered.

Then he told them, "Give the Emperor what belongs to him and give God what belongs to God." Jesus' enemies could not catch him saying anything wrong there in front of the people. They were amazed at his answer and kept quiet.

Life in the Future World

The Sadducees didn't believe that people would rise to life after death. So some of them came to Jesus and said:

Teacher, Moses wrote that if a married man dies and has no children, his brother should marry the widow. Their first son would then be thought of as the son of the dead brother.

There were once seven brothers. The first one married, but died without having any children. The second one married his brother's widow, and he also died without having any children. The same thing happened to the third one. Finally, all seven brothers married that woman and died without having any children.

At last the woman died. When God raises people from death, whose wife will this woman be? All seven brothers had married her.

Jesus answered:

The people in this world get married. But in the future world no one who is worthy to rise from death will either marry or die. They will be like the angels and will be God's children, because they have been raised to life.

In the story about the burning bush, Moses clearly shows that people will live again. He said, "The Lord is the God worshipped by Abraham, Isaac, and Jacob." So the Lord isn't the God of the dead, but of the living. This means that everyone is alive as far as God is concerned.

Some of the teachers of the Law of Moses said, "Teacher, you have given a good answer!" From then on, no one dared to ask Jesus any questions.

About David's Son

Jesus asked, "Why do people say that the Messiah will be the son of King David? In the book of Psalms, David himself says,

'The Lord said to my Lord,
Sit at my right side
until I make your enemies
into a footstool for you.'
David spoke of the Messiah as his Lord, so how can the Messiah be his son?"

Jesus and the Teachers of the Law of Moses

While everyone was listening to Jesus, he said to his disciples:

Guard against the teachers of the Law of Moses! They love to walk around in long robes, and they like to be greeted in the market. They want the front seats in the meeting places and the best seats at banquets. But they cheat widows out of their homes and then pray long prayers just to show off. These teachers will be punished most of all.

"No rain,
no mushrooms.
No God,
no world."
African proverb

> "A great many people think that they are thinking when they are merely rearranging their prejudices."
>
> *William James*

A Widow's Offering

Jesus looked up and saw some rich people tossing their gifts into the offering box. He also saw a poor widow putting in two cents. And he said, "I tell you that this poor woman has put in more than all the others. Everyone else gave what they didn't need. But she is very poor and gave everything she had."

The Temple Will Be Destroyed

Some people were talking about the beautiful stones used to build the temple and about the gifts that had been placed in it. Jesus said, "Do you see these stones? The time is coming when not one of them will be left in place. They will all be knocked down."

Warning about Trouble

Some people asked, "Teacher, when will all this happen? How can we know when these things are about to take place?"

Jesus replied:

Don't be fooled by those who will come and claim to be me. They will say, "I am Christ!" and "Now is the time!" But don't follow them. When you hear about wars and riots, don't

be afraid. These things will have to happen first, but that isn't the end.

Nations will go to war against one another, and kingdoms will attack each other. There will be great earthquakes, and in many places people will starve to death and suffer terrible diseases. All sorts of frightening things will be seen in the sky.

Before all this happens, you will be arrested and punished. You will be tried in your meeting places and put in jail. Because of me you will be placed on trial before kings and governors. But this will be your chance to tell about your faith.

Don't worry about what you will say to defend yourselves. I will give you the wisdom to know what to say. None of your enemies will be able to oppose you or to say that you are wrong. You will be betrayed by your own parents, brothers, family, and friends. Some of you will even be killed. Because of me, you will be hated by everyone. But don't worry! You will be saved by being faithful to me.

Jerusalem Will Be Destroyed

When you see Jerusalem surrounded by soldiers, you will know that it will soon be destroyed. If you are living in Judea at that time, run to the mountains. If you are in the city, leave it. And if you are out in the country, don't go back into the city. This time of

"The sky and the earth won't last for ever"

punishment is what is written about in the Scriptures. It will be an awful time for women who are expecting babies or nursing young children! Everywhere in the land people will suffer horribly and be punished. Some of them will be killed by swords. Others will be carried off to foreign countries. Jerusalem will be overrun by foreign nations until their time comes to an end.

When the Son of Man Appears

Strange things will happen to the sun, moon, and stars.

The nations on earth will be afraid of the roaring sea and tides, and they won't know what to do. People will be so frightened that they will faint because of what is happening to the world. Every power in the sky will be shaken. Then the Son of Man will be seen, coming in a cloud with great power and glory. When all of this starts happening, stand up straight and be brave. You will soon be set free.

A Lesson from a Fig Tree
Then Jesus told them a story:
When you see a fig tree or any other tree putting out leaves, you know that summer will soon come. So, when you see these things happening, you know that God's kingdom will soon be here. You can be sure that some of the people of this generation will still be alive when all of this takes place. The sky and the earth won't last for ever, but my words will.

A Warning
Don't spend all of your time thinking about eating or drinking or worrying about life. If you do, the final day will suddenly catch you like a trap. That day will surprise everyone on earth. Watch out and keep praying that you can escape all that is going to happen and that the Son of Man will be pleased with you.
Jesus taught in the temple each day, and he spent each night on the Mount of Olives. Everyone got up early and came to the temple to hear him teach.

Life Story

JON DAVIES

"It was the evidence for the resurrection which finally sealed it for me. If Jesus could do that then he could do anything."

Jon Davies is a barrister.

"I was invited to a 'Christians in Sport' dinner held at the rugby club. This started getting me more interested in the Christian faith. However, the most important step for me was the 'Alpha' course – a series for sceptics, put on by the parish church. I was genuinely curious about the subject matter. I had never studied the basics of Christianity before really to know if it was worth pursuing. However, I never doubted the existence of Jesus, and for me the wealth of history and archaeology was very convincing. It was more the significance of who Jesus was and what he said that raised questions for me. After the course I came to the point where I could understand the Christian faith intellectually, but I was reluctant to make a personal commitment. In the end I realised that there is no middle ground and I entrusted my life to Christ."

"I have spent my whole working life arguing other people's cases. It hasn't mattered whether I believed them or not because the ultimate responsibility of whether it's true is not mine but that of the judge or jury. I don't have to make that decision. However, the decision to become a Christian was one which only I could make. It was more than just seeing the arguments. I now find myself arguing for someone and something I really believe in."

GET RID OF HIM

The Festival of Thin Bread, also called Passover*, was near. The chief priests and the teachers of the Law of Moses were looking for a way to get rid of Jesus, because they were afraid of what the people might do.

Then Satan entered the heart of Judas Iscariot, who was one of the twelve apostles.

Judas went to talk with the chief priests and the officers of the temple police about how he could help them arrest Jesus. They were very pleased and offered to pay Judas some money. He agreed and started looking for a good chance to betray Jesus when the crowds were not around.

Jesus Eats with His Disciples
The day had come for the Festival of Thin Bread, and it was time to kill the Passover lambs. So Jesus said to Peter and John, "Go and prepare the Passover meal for us to eat."

But they asked, "Where do you want us to prepare it?"

Jesus told them, "As you go into the city, you will meet a man carrying a jar of water. Follow him into the house and say to the owner, 'Our teacher wants to know where he can eat the Passover meal with his disciples.' The owner will take you upstairs and show you a large room ready for you to use. Prepare the meal there."

Peter and John left. They found everything just as Jesus had told them, and they prepared the Passover meal.

The Lord's Supper

When the time came for Jesus and the apostles to eat, he said to them, "I have very much wanted to eat this Passover meal with you before I suffer. I tell you that I won't eat another Passover meal until it is finally eaten in God's kingdom."

Jesus took a cup of wine in his hands and gave thanks to God. Then he told the apostles, "Take this wine and share it with each other. I tell you that I won't drink any more wine until God's kingdom comes."

Jesus took some bread in his hands and gave thanks for it. He broke the bread and handed it to his apostles. Then he said, "This is my body, which is given for you. Eat this as a way of remembering me!"

After the meal he took another cup of wine in his hands. Then he said, "This is my blood. It is poured out for you, and with it God makes his new agreement. The one who will betray me is here at the table with me! The Son of Man will die in the way that has been decided for him, but it will be terrible for the one who betrays him!"

Then the apostles started arguing about who would ever do such a thing.

An Argument about Greatness

The apostles got into an argument about which one of them was the greatest. So Jesus told them:

Foreign kings order their people around, and powerful rulers call themselves everyone's friends. But don't be like them. The most important one of you should be like the least important, and your leader should be like a servant. Who do people think is the greatest, a person who is served or one who serves? Isn't it the one who is served? But I have been with you as a servant.

You have stayed with me in all my troubles. So I will give you the right to rule as kings, just as my Father has given me the right to rule as a king. You will eat and drink with me in my kingdom, and you will each sit on a throne to judge the tribes of Israel.

Jesus' Disciples Will Be Tested

Jesus said, "Simon, listen to me! Satan has demanded the right to test each one of you, as a farmer does when he separates wheat from the husks. But Simon, I've prayed that your faith will be strong. And when you've come back to me, help the others."

Peter said, "Lord, I'm ready to go with you to jail and even to die with you."

Jesus replied, "Peter, I tell you that before a rooster crows tomorrow morning, you will say three times that you don't know me."

Moneybags, Travelling Bags, and Swords

Jesus asked his disciples, "When I sent you out without a moneybag or a travelling bag or sandals, did you need anything?"

"No!" they answered.

Jesus told them, "But now, if you've got a moneybag, take it with you. Also take a travelling bag, and if you haven't got a sword, sell some

* PASSOVER

The Passover was an annual religious festival to commemorate how God had rescued the Jewish nation from slavery in Egypt. The Old Testament records how the angel of death killed the first-born child in every Egyptian home, but "passed over" the Hebrew homes that had lamb's blood sprinkled on their doors. This blood was a sign of that family's trust that God would rescue them. That event persuaded the Egyptian Pharaoh to let the people of Israel go free. This Old Testament example of God's rescue is a picture of the sacrificial death of Jesus. In this case, the blood (or death) of Jesus would save men and women of any nation from the natural consequences of being enslaved to their own self-centredness.

of your clothes and buy one. Do this because the Scriptures say, 'He was considered a criminal.' This was written about me, and it will soon come true."

The disciples said, "Lord, here are two swords!"

"Enough of that!" Jesus replied.

Jesus Prays

Jesus went out to the Mount of Olives, as he often did, and his disciples went with him. When they got there, he told them, "Pray that you won't be tested."

Jesus walked on a little way before he knelt down and prayed, "Father, if you will, please don't make me suffer by making me drink from this cup. But do what you want, and not what I want."

Then an angel from heaven came to help him. Jesus was in great pain and prayed so sincerely that his sweat fell to the ground like drops of blood.

Jesus got up from praying and went over to his disciples. They were asleep and worn out from being so sad. He said to them, "Why are you asleep? Wake up and pray that you won't be tested."

Jesus Is Arrested

While Jesus was still speaking, a crowd came up. It was led by Judas, one of the twelve apostles. He went over to Jesus and greeted him with a kiss.

Jesus asked Judas, "Are you betraying the Son of Man with a kiss?"

When Jesus' disciples saw what was about to happen, they asked, "Lord, should we attack them with a sword?" One of the disciples even struck at the high priest's servant with his sword and cut off the servant's right ear.

"Enough of that!" Jesus said. Then he touched the servant's ear and healed it.

Jesus spoke to the

chief priests, the temple police, and the leaders who had come to arrest him. He said, "Why do you come out with swords and clubs and treat me like a criminal? I was with you every day in the temple, and you didn't arrest me. But this is your time, and darkness is in control."

Peter Says He Doesn't Know Jesus

Jesus was arrested and led away to the house of the high priest, while Peter followed at a distance. Some people built a fire in the middle of the courtyard and were sitting around it. Peter sat there with them, and a servant girl saw him. Then after she had looked at him carefully, she said, "This man was with Jesus!"

Peter said, "Woman, I don't even know that man!"

A little later someone else saw Peter and said, "You're one of them!"

About an hour later another man insisted, "This man must have been with Jesus. They both come from Galilee."

Peter replied, "I don't know what you are talking about!" At once, while Peter was still speaking, a rooster crowed.

The Lord turned and

looked at Peter. And Peter remembered that the Lord had said, "Before a rooster crows tomorrow morning, you will say three times that you don't know me." Then Peter went out and cried hard.

The men who were guarding Jesus made fun of him and beat him. They put a blindfold on him and said, "Tell us who struck you!" They kept on insulting Jesus in many other ways.

Jesus Is Questioned by the Council

At daybreak the nation's leaders, the chief priests, and the teachers of the Law of Moses got together and brought Jesus before their council. They said, "Tell us! Are you the Messiah?"

Jesus replied, "If I said so, you wouldn't believe me. And if I asked you a question, you wouldn't answer. But from now on, the Son of Man will be seated at the right side of God All-Powerful."

Then they asked, "Are you the Son of God?"

Jesus answered, "You say I am!"

They replied, "Why do we need more witnesses? He said it himself!"

Pilate Questions Jesus

Everyone in the council got up and led Jesus off to Pilate. They started accusing him and said, "We caught this man trying to get our people to riot and to stop paying taxes to the Emperor. He also claims that he is the Messiah, our king."

Pilate asked Jesus, "Are you the king of the Jews?"

"Those are your words," Jesus answered.

Pilate told the chief priests and the crowd, "I don't find him guilty of anything."

But they all kept on saying, "He's been teaching and causing trouble all over Judea. He started in Galilee and has now come all the way here."

Jesus Is Brought before Herod

When Pilate heard this, he asked, "Is this man from Galilee?" After Pilate learned that Jesus came from the region ruled by Herod, he sent him to Herod, who was in Jerusalem at that time.

For a long time Herod had wanted to see Jesus and was very happy because he finally had this chance. He had heard many things about Jesus and hoped to see him work a miracle.

Herod asked him a lot of questions, but Jesus didn't answer. Then the chief priests and the teachers of the Law of Moses stood up and accused him of all kinds of bad things.

Herod and his soldiers made fun of Jesus and insulted him. They put a fine robe on him and sent him back to Pilate. That same day Herod and Pilate became friends, even though they had been enemies before this.

The Death Sentence

Pilate called together the chief priests, the leaders, and the people. He told them, "You brought Jesus to me and said he was a troublemaker. But I've questioned him here in front of you, and I haven't

found him guilty of anything that you say he has done. Herod didn't find him guilty either and sent him back. This man doesn't deserve to be put to death! I'll just have him beaten with a whip and set free."

But the whole crowd shouted, "Kill Jesus! Give us Barabbas!" Now Barabbas was in jail because he had started a riot in the city and had murdered someone.

Pilate wanted to set Jesus free, so he spoke again to the crowds.

But they kept shouting, "Nail him to a cross! Nail him to a cross!"

Pilate spoke to them a third time, "But what crime has he done? I haven't found him guilty of anything for which he should be put to death. I'll have him beaten with a whip and set free."

The people kept on shouting as loud as they could for Jesus to be put to death. Finally, Pilate gave in. He freed

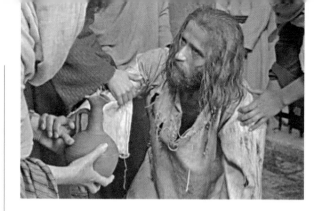

> "Learn as if you were going to live forever. Live as if you were going to die tomorrow."
> *Mahatma Gandhi*

the man who was in jail for rioting and murder, because he was the one the crowd wanted to be set free. Then Pilate handed Jesus over for them to do what they wanted with him.

Jesus Is Nailed to a Cross*
As Jesus was being led away, some soldiers grabbed hold of a man from Cyrene named Simon. He was coming in from the fields, but they put the cross on him and made him carry it behind Jesus.

A large crowd was following Jesus, and in the crowd a lot of women were crying and weeping for him. Jesus turned to the women and said:

Women of Jerusalem, don't cry for me! Cry for yourselves and for your children. Some day people will say, "Women who never had children are really fortunate!" At that time everyone will say to the mountains, "Fall on us!" They will say to the hills, "Hide us!" If this can happen when the wood is green, what do you think will happen when it is dry?

Two criminals were led out to be put to death with Jesus. When the soldiers came to the place called "The Skull," they nailed Jesus to a cross. They also nailed the two criminals to crosses, one on each side of Jesus.

Jesus said, "Father, forgive these people! They don't know what they're doing."

While the crowd stood there watching Jesus, the soldiers gambled for his clothes. The leaders insulted him by saying, "He saved others. Now he should save himself, if he really is God's chosen Messiah!"

The soldiers made fun of Jesus and brought him some wine. They said, "If you're the king of the Jews, save yourself!"

Above him was a sign that

"Forgive these people! They don't know what they're doing"

said, "This is the King of the Jews."

One of the criminals hanging there also insulted Jesus by saying, "Aren't you the Messiah? Save yourself and save us!"

But the other criminal told the first one off, "Don't you fear God? Aren't you getting the same punishment as this man? We got what was

* CROSS

The Roman punishment of crucifixion was one of the most terrible forms of execution invented by man. The person who was going to die had to carry his own wooden cross beam. The upright post was already in the ground. The victim was stripped, his wrists tied and sometimes nailed to the wooden beam before it was lifted up and fixed to the upright. The feet were tied or nailed to the cross. A notice with the name of the person, his home town and his crime was fixed to the cross. It was an agonising punishment and usually brought death by slow suffocation. It often took hours or even days to die.

coming to us, but he didn't do anything wrong." Then he said to Jesus, "Remember me when you come into power!"

Jesus replied, "I promise that today you will be with me in paradise."

The Death of Jesus

Around midday the sky turned dark and stayed that way until the middle of the afternoon. The sun stopped shining, and the curtain in the temple split down the middle. Jesus shouted, "Father, I put myself in your hands!" Then he died.

When the Roman officer saw what had happened, he praised God and said, "Jesus must really have been a good man!"

A crowd had gathered to see the terrible sight. Then after they had seen it, they

felt broken-hearted and went home. All of Jesus' close friends and the women who had come with him from Galilee stood at a distance and watched.

Jesus Is Buried

There was a man named Joseph, who was from Arimathea in Judea. Joseph was a good and honest man, and he was eager for God's kingdom to come. He was also a member of the council, but he didn't agree with what they had decided.

Joseph went to Pilate and asked for Jesus' body. He took the body down from the cross and wrapped it in fine cloth. Then he put it in a tomb that had been cut out of solid rock and had never been used. It was Friday, and the Sabbath was about to begin.

The women who had come with Jesus from Galilee followed Joseph and watched how Jesus' body was placed in the tomb. Then they went to prepare some sweet-smelling spices for his burial. But on the Sabbath they rested, as the Law of Moses commands.

DEATH DEFEATED

Very early on Sunday morning the women went to the tomb, carrying the spices that they had prepared. When they found the stone rolled away from the entrance, they went in.

But they didn't find the body of the Lord Jesus, and they didn't know what to think.

Suddenly two men in shining white clothes stood beside them. The women were afraid and bowed to the ground. But the men said, "Why are you looking in the place of the dead for someone who is alive? Jesus isn't here! He's been raised from death. Remember that while he was still in Galilee, he told you, 'The Son of Man will be

"They didn't find the body"

handed over to sinners who will nail him to a cross. But three days later he will rise to life.'" Then they remembered what Jesus had said.

Mary Magdalene, Joanna, Mary the mother of James, and some other women were the ones who had gone to the tomb. When they returned, they told the eleven apostles and the others what had happened. The apostles thought it was all nonsense, and they wouldn't believe.

But Peter ran to the tomb. And when he stooped down

and looked in, he saw only the burial clothes. Then he returned, wondering what had happened.

Jesus Appears to Two Disciples

That same day two of Jesus' disciples were going to the village of Emmaus, which was about 11 kilometres from Jerusalem. As they were talking and thinking about what had happened, Jesus came near and started walking along beside them. But they didn't know who he was.

Jesus asked them, "What were you talking about as you walked along?"

The two of them stood there looking sad and gloomy. Then the one named Cleopas asked Jesus, "Are you the only person from Jerusalem who doesn't know what was happening there these last few days?"

"What do you mean?" Jesus asked.

They answered:

Those things that happened to Jesus from Nazareth. By what he did and said he showed that he was a powerful prophet, who pleased God and all the people. Then the chief priests and our leaders had him arrested and sentenced to die on a cross. We had hoped that he would be the one to set

"How can you be so slow to believe?"

Israel free! But it has already been three days since all this happened.

Some women in our group surprised us. They had gone to the tomb early in the morning, but didn't find the body of Jesus. They came back, saying that they had seen a vision of angels who told them that he is alive. Some men from our group went to the tomb and found it just as the women had said. But they didn't see Jesus either.

Then Jesus asked the two disciples, "Why can't you understand? How can you be so slow to believe all that the prophets said? Didn't you know that the Messiah would have to suffer before he was given his glory?" Jesus then explained everything written about himself in the Scriptures, beginning with the Law of Moses and the Books of the Prophets.

When the two of them came near the village where they were going, Jesus seemed to be going further. They begged him, "Stay with us! It's already late, and the sun is going down." So Jesus went into the house to stay with them.

After Jesus sat down to eat, he took some bread. He blessed it and broke it. Then

he gave it to them. At once they knew who he was, but he disappeared. They said to each other, "When he talked with us along the road and explained the Scriptures to us, didn't it warm our hearts?" So they got straight up and returned to Jerusalem.

The two disciples found the eleven apostles and the others gathered together. And they learnt from the group that the Lord was really alive and had appeared to Peter. Then the disciples from Emmaus told them what happened on the road and how they knew he was the Lord when he broke the bread.

What Jesus' Followers Must Do

While Jesus' disciples were talking about what had happened, Jesus appeared and greeted them. They were frightened and terrified because they thought they were seeing a ghost.

But Jesus said, "Why are you so frightened? Why do you doubt? Look at my hands and my feet and see who I am! Touch me and find out for yourselves. Ghosts don't have flesh and bones as you see I have."

After Jesus said this, he showed them his hands and his feet. The disciples were so glad and amazed that they couldn't believe it. Jesus then asked them, "Have you got something to eat?" They gave him a piece of baked fish. He took it and ate it as they watched.

Jesus said to them, "While I was still with you, I told you that everything written about me in the Law of Moses, the Books of the Prophets, and in the Psalms had to happen."

Then he helped them understand the Scriptures. He told them:

The Scriptures say that the Messiah must suffer, then three days later he will rise from death. They also say that all people of every nation must be told in my name to turn to God, in order to be forgiven. So beginning in Jerusalem, you must tell everyone everything that has happened. I will send you the one my Father has promised, but you must stay in the city until you are given power from heaven.

Jesus Returns to Heaven

Jesus led his disciples out to Bethany, where he raised his hands and blessed them. As he was doing this, he left and was taken up to heaven. After his disciples had worshipped him, they returned to Jerusalem and were very happy. They spent their time in the temple, praising God.

DID JESUS RISE FROM THE DEAD?

The resurrection of Jesus brought about a remarkable change in the first Christians. From the very beginning it had a vital place in their message. It changed Jesus' apparent defeat on the cross into a great victory over death. For Christians Jesus' resurrection is the foundation of their faith.

But is there any evidence that Jesus rose from the dead? Actually, the resurrection is one of the most well-attested events in history. Investigators have set out to debunk the resurrection claim – and have ended up by becoming convinced that it actually happened. Many lawyers have considered the evidence for believing that Jesus rose again, and have concluded that this evidence is stronger than most that is accepted in a court of law.

Consider the following:

- The description of Jesus' crucifixion leaves no doubt that he died on the cross.

- The sealing of the tomb would have prevented any half-dead human from escaping.

- If the tomb had not been empty, why didn't the authorities simply produce the body?

- If the disciples stole the body, why were they prepared to die for their belief in his resurrection when they knew it to be a lie?

- If their claim to have seen Jesus was no more than an hallucination, how do we explain the empty tomb?

- Whatever happened must also explain why a band of dejected and defeated followers, who had witnessed the execution of their leader, were prepared a few days later to stand up boldly in the same city in which he had died and declare that he was risen from the dead.

The former Lord Chief Justice, Lord Darling, once said: "There exists such overwhelming evidence, positive and negative, factual and circumstantial, that no intelligent jury in the world would fail to bring in a verdict that the resurrection story is true."

FACT:	THE TOMB WAS EMPTY				
POSSIBLE EXPLANATION	The disciples stole the body	They went to the wrong tomb	The Jews or Romans stole the body	Jesus didn't really die	Jesus had risen
OBJECTION	But then they gave their lives for what they knew to be a lie	But then the Jews or Romans would have pointed out their mistake	But then they would have produced the body to silence the Christians	He would have had to move a 2 ton stone and overcome trained Roman guards by himself	?

FACT:	THE DISCIPLES CLAIMED TO SEE JESUS				
POSSIBLE EXPLANATION	They made it up	They saw a ghost	It was an illusion	Jesus couldn't have been resurrected because such things don't happen	Jesus had risen
OBJECTION	But then why were a dejected band of followers so transformed?	But they could touch him and he ate with them	But 500 people don't all see the same illusion at the same time	Just because something only happens once 'unscientific' on doesn't make it	?

KNOWING GOD PERSONALLY

We live in a world where many are pessimistic about the future. The media hype has done little to persuade us that life will be better in the third millennium. The problems of crime, violence, economic uncertainty and human suffering show little sign of going away. Against this background, Jesus Christ offers real hope. He highlights our basic need to find peace with God. He then makes such reconciliation possible.

GOD LOVES YOU AND WANTS YOU TO KNOW HIM

HOW CAN YOU KNOW GOD LOVES YOU?
'God loved the people of this world so much that he gave his only Son, so that everyone who has faith in him will have eternal life and never really die.' *John 3:16*

WHAT IS ETERNAL LIFE?
'Eternal life is to know you, the only true God, and to know Jesus Christ, the one you sent.' *John 17:3*

Why is it that most people do not know God in this way?

WE CHOOSE TO GO OUR OWN WAY, CUTTING OURSELVES OFF FROM GOD

WE ARE EACH RESPONSIBLE
We prefer to go our own way instead of God's; we may openly disobey God who made us, or simply ignore him. It's this self-centred attitude that the Bible calls 'sin'.

WE ARE ALL THE SAME
'All of us have sinned and fallen short of God's glory.' *Romans 3:23*

WE EACH SUFFER THE EFFECTS
'That way of living leads to certain spiritual death.' *Romans 8:13*

God is perfect, we are sinful, so there is a great gap between us. We may try to feel better through work, relationships, sport or religion. But all our attempts fail, because we have ignored the real problem – turning our back on God.

The third point gives us the only answer to this problem...

God

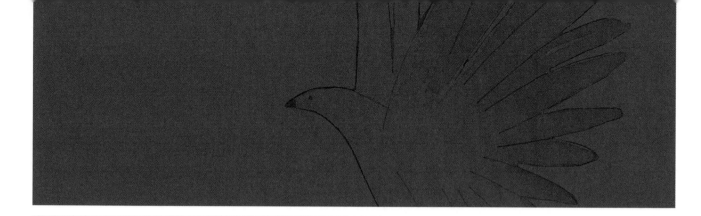

BY GIVING HIS LIFE FOR US, JESUS CHRIST OPENED UP THE ONLY WAY TO FRIENDSHIP WITH GOD

JESUS IS UNIQUE
'I am the way, the truth and the life!' Jesus answered. 'Without me, no-one can go to the Father.' *John 14:6*

JESUS HAS THE POWER TO PUT THINGS RIGHT
'While we were his enemies, Christ reconciled us to God by dying for us.' *Colossians 1:21,22*

JESUS HAS POWER OVER DEATH
'For forty days after Jesus had suffered and died, he proved in many ways that he had been raised from death. He appeared to his apostles and spoke to them about God's kingdom.' *Acts 1:3*

Jesus took the consequences of our self-centredness by giving up his life on the cross. He proved he had broken sin's destructive power by rising from the dead. Jesus offers us freedom from guilt and a bridge back to God.

It's not enough just to know all this...

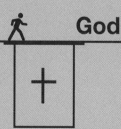

WE NEED TO ACCEPT JESUS CHRIST, SO WE CAN KNOW GOD'S FORGIVENESS AND FRIENDSHIP

WE NEED TO ACCEPT JESUS CHRIST
'Some people accepted him and put their faith in him. So he gave them the right to be the children of God' *John 1:12*

ACCEPTING JESUS CHRIST INVOLVES:

1 Agreeing with God that we are to blame for turning our back on him

2 Trusting God to forgive us completely because Jesus has paid the price for our self-centredness

3 Choosing to follow Jesus

JESUS GIVES THIS PICTURE

'Listen! I am standing and knocking at your door. If you hear my voice and open the door, I will come in and we will eat together.' *Revelation 3:20*

It's not enough just to know or feel that these things are true. We have a choice to make...

THESE ILLUSTRATIONS DESCRIBE TWO KINDS OF PEOPLE

SELF-CENTRED PERSON
- Self in the driving seat
- Jesus Christ outside
- Interests centred on self, often resulting in discord and frustration

CHRIST-CENTRED PERSON
- Jesus Christ in the driving seat
- Self following Jesus Christ, drawing on his life and power
- Interests centred on Christ, resulting in growing harmony with God's purpose

Which illustration better describes you?
Which illustration would you like to describe you?

TO ACCEPT JESUS CHRIST, YOU MUST PUT YOUR LIFE IN HIS HANDS. GOD IS NOT SO CONCERNED WITH YOUR WORDS AS HE IS WITH YOUR ATTITUDE. HERE IS SOMETHING YOU COULD SAY TO HIM:

'Lord Jesus, I am sorry that I have been going my own way. Thank you for paying the price of my self-centredness by dying on the cross. Please come and take first place in my life. Make me the kind of person you want me to be.'

COULD YOU SAY THIS TO GOD AND MEAN IT?
Why not say this to God now?
Jesus Christ will come into your life as he promised.

WHAT HAPPENS WHEN YOU PUT YOUR TRUST IN JESUS CHRIST?

IF YOU HAVE INVITED JESUS CHRIST INTO YOUR LIFE, MANY THINGS HAVE HAPPENED, INCLUDING:

1 Jesus Christ has come into your life by his spirit and he will never leave you
   Revelation 3:20; Hebrews 13:5

2 You have been forgiven completely
   Colossians 2:14

3 You have a new power in your life, enabling you to change *Colossians 2:15*

4 You can begin to experience life with God as he intended *John 17:3; John 10:10*

HOW CAN YOU BE SURE ALL THIS HAS REALLY HAPPENED?

YOU CAN KNOW THAT JESUS CHRIST IS IN YOUR LIFE BECAUSE GOD HAS PROMISED AND HE CAN BE TRUSTED
'God has said that he gave us eternal life and that this life comes to us from his Son. And so, if we have God's Son, we have his life. But if we don't have the Son, we don't have this life. All of you have faith in the Son of God and I have written to let you know that you have eternal life.'
1 John 5:11-13

'Thank God often that Jesus Christ is in your life and that he will never leave you.' *Romans 8:38,39*

You can know that the spirit of Christ lives in you and that you have eternal life from the moment you invited Christ into your life, because this is what he has promised.

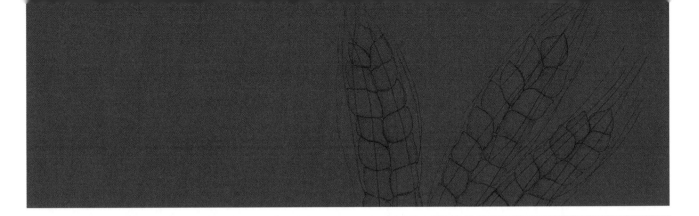

WHAT ABOUT FEELINGS?

DO NOT DEPEND ON HOW YOU FEEL
We can always rely on God and his promises
in the Bible. But we cannot always rely on our
feelings. Because of this, the Christian lives by
trusting God and what he has said through the
Bible, rather than by trusting feelings, which may
come and go.

FACT	FAITH	FEELING
God and his word the Bible	*Our trust in God and his word*	*The results of trusting God*

It would be impossible for the guard's van to pull
the train. In the same way, it is important to rely
on God and what he has said in the Bible, and not
be pushed around by our feelings. Just as the coal
needs to be put into the engine from the coal
truck in order for the train to run, so we need to
put our trust in God's word.

SUGGESTIONS FOR CHRISTIAN GROWTH

OUR FAITH IN GOD GROWS AS WE TRUST GOD
WITH EVERY DETAIL OF OUR LIVES. YOU WILL FIND
IT HELPFUL TO:

- **G**et to know God by reading the Bible
  2 Timothy 3:14-17
- **R**espond to God in prayer *Philippians 4:6*
- **O**bey God moment by moment *Luke 6:46-49*
- **W**alk in the power of the Holy Spirit
  Colossians 2:6; Ephesians 3:14-21, 5:18
- **T**ell others about Jesus Christ by life and words
  *Matthew 28:18-20; 2 Corinthians 5:17-20;
  Ephesians 4:1*
- **H**ave contact with other Christians
  Hebrews 10:25; Acts 2:42-47

Several coals burn brightly together; but put one aside
and its fire goes out. In the same way, it is very hard
to live the Christian life by yourself. Go to a church
where Jesus is worshipped and the Bible is taught, and
join others who have come to know God personally
and are growing in their relationship with him.

Explore what it might be like to take a step of faith on
www.rejesus.co.uk/encounters

Talk with others online on www.rejesus.co.uk/community

Acknowledgements

This magazine is the result of co-operation between:

Agapé,
Fairgate House, Kings Road,
Tyseley, Birmingham B11 2AA.
Phone: 0121 765 4404
Email: info@agape.org.uk

Deo Gloria Trust,
Selsdon House,
212/220 Addington Road,
South Croydon CR2 8LD.
Phone: 020 8651 6246
Email: resources@deo-gloria.co.uk

There Is Hope,
67 Wright St, Hull,
East Yorkshire HU2 8JD.
Phone: 01482 606606
Email: david@hope.karoo.co.uk

Editorial Team
David Hill, Tim Harding, John Arkell, Janet Denison, Roger Vann, Andrew Taylor & Tony Brown

Design & Print Management
Yeomans Press
The Hop Farm Country Park,
Paddock Wood, Kent TN12 6PY
Phone: 01622 870095

Photography
Photographs illustrating the story are taken from the JESUS film © Copyright Inspirational Films. Taken from Luke's report, JESUS has been viewed by some 2 billion people in over 900 languages. Scenes from this most authentic film help bring Luke's words to life.

Photographs of Israel today are taken from the DVD of So, Who Is This Jesus? © Copyright Christian Television Association.

ISBN 0 9522218 1 0

Copyright © 1998 / 2001 / 2005

The account of the life of Jesus is taken from Luke's Gospel in the Contemporary English Version (CEV). Published with kind permission from The National Bible Society of Scotland,
7 Hampton Terrace, Edinburgh EH12 5XU. Text © American Bible Society, 1991. Anglicised text © The National Bible Society of Scotland, 1997

Quotations from the Bible on the back cover are taken from: The Anglicised text of the Contemporary English Version (CEV). Published with kind permission from The National Bible Society of Scotland. Text © The National Bible Society of Scotland, 1997.

The Message – Scripture taken from THE MESSAGE. Copyright © by Eugene H. Peterson, 1993, 1994, 1995. Used by permission of NavPress Publishing Group.

Quotations from the Bible on the Knowing God Personally pages are taken from the Contemporary English Version New Testament, © American Bible Society 1991, 1992, 1995, used by permission / Anglicisation © British & Foreign Bible Society 1996 and from the New International Version © International Bible Society 1973, 1978, 1984. Published by Hodder & Stoughton and used by permission.